Women, Sex and

In Their Own Words

Liz Evans

Pandora
An Imprint of HarperCollins*Publishers*

LIZ EVANS has been a freelance journalist since 1988, when she began
r   appeared in the *Guardian*,
    MAIN   d *Elle*. She lives in a noisy
    781.6608 Evans, Liz.   very large, rather violent
        Women, sex and   her first book.
        rock'n'roll :

    31143005366746
                                              c.l

Pandora
An Imprint of HarperCollins*Publishers*
77–85 Fulham Palace Road
Hammersmith, London W6 8JB
1160 Battery Street
San Francisco, California 94111–1213

Published by Pandora © 1994

10 9 8 7 6 5 4 3 2 1

A catalogue record for this book
is available from the British Library

ISBN 0 04 440900 1

Printed in Great Britain by The Bath Press, Bath, Avon

Contents

Acknowledgements

I would like to thank Dominic Wills and Marlon for love and support. Also my family, my mother Joan Evans, brother Ted and sister Katy.

Thanks to all my friends: my flatmate Dawn Thistelton, everyone from Cheltenham, especially Julie Whittle-Slater, Hilary Dyer, Martin Williams, James Robins, Guy Edwards and Leese Collier, Sonya Dunsdon, Andy Smith and little Lottie Dunsdon-Smith, Jon Best and Miki Berenyi, Sandra Van Der Feen, Pinkie Maclure, Helen Utidjian, Steve and Liz in New York, Peter, Joan and Colin Metz in Boston, Annie and Chris, Caroline McCarthy in New Zealand, and Steve and Kristina in Australia.

I am indebted to my agent Carol Heaton and my editors at Pandora, Karen Holden and Belinda Budge. Also, all the publicity and management people: Lee Ellen Newman at East West, Diane at Eligible, Eugene Manzi and Juliet Sensicle at London Records, Colleen and Tony at 4AD, Tamra and Gary Smith at Fort Apache, Billy O'Connell at Throwing Management, Christina Kyriacon and Nettie Walker at One Little Indian Records, John Best and Phil Savage, Lisa Paulon, Rob Partridge, Neil Storey, Michael at Gold Mountain Entertainment, Billy Chainsaw, Patsy at Rough Trade, Nick at Island Records and Richard Gordon. And respect and gratitude to all the photographers: Tom 'Chap' Sheehan, Matt Bright, Stephen Sweet, Joe Dilworth, Adrian Boot, Phil Nicholls, Piers Alladyce, Andy Catlin and Steve Gullick.

And finally thanks to Claire Dowse, Paul Elliott and especially Phil Alexander of *Kerrang!* magazine for work, beer and ridiculousness.

Introduction

While women undeniably have a history in rock, their impact has been carefully reduced by their representation. The media and the music industry have packaged women together in blips and starts of female interruption, slotting them into little niches where they fade as individuals for the sake of the stereotype. Helpless victims, dizzy sex queens, earth mothers and femme fatales have knocked female power off centre, hidden female experience behind publicly acceptable or manageable moulds, and deadened the significance of female rock culture since its inception.

Over the last five or six years, the women interviewed in this book and their contemporaries have fiercely begun to defy the traps laid down for them by rewriting their starring roles and ripping up the infrastructure of male rock tradition. Artistically, these women share little in common, but collectively their efforts have shaken the foundations of a once safe sanctuary for rattled male egos, and blasted open the faultline initiated by a scattered heritage of visionaries and rulebreakers.

Janis Joplin flouted gender restrictions in the late 1960s with her irrepressible appetites, outspoken sassiness and feisty impassioned performances, while Joni Mitchell dealt with the contradictions and complexities of irrational female emotion. Patti Smith rode in with punk during the 1970s, mixing poetry and rock music with a severely confrontational androgynous image. Siouxsie Sioux experimented with adornment and masks, again trampling orthodox ideas of femininity, while Chrissie Hynde fronted her band clutching a guitar with a powerfully cool confidence. Kate Bush survived her initial sex symbol treatment and took her wildly imaginative and highly original creativity into the 1980s, developing into a technically proficient, self-contained unit, building her own studio and employing her family to look after her business, while Annie Lennox adopted cross dressing as a way of avoiding obvious female roles.

All of these women—and of course there were many others: The Slits, The Raincoats, The Au Pairs, Debbie Harry, Yoko Ono and Grace Jones, to name but a few more—dared to make a difference in their own way. Their achievements have often been distorted and their significance questioned. They've been compared with each other and with more recent artists, they've been judged en masse and clotted together beneath the distasteful and condescending title of Women in Rock; in short, they've been robbed of their individuality. But the truth is they have mapped out female rock culture for the last thirty years and have provided the increasingly unlimited frame of reference in which today's female rock artists operate.

Despite three decades of female rock activity, and the recent eruption of female anger, aggression, sexuality and pain, rock's male-dominated arena is still riddled with stubborn attitudes, and the basic inability to fully understand female emotion, ordinary experience and inner lives, which disables women songwriters and musicians. Certain factions who have aligned themselves with the recent trend for political correctness, particularly the music press, seem to believe that they have a handle on the current situation, but their clumsy, and often patronising treatment of female artists speaks for itself.

Full integration of female perspectives will not happen until the stereotypes are slaughtered and buried, and personal female self-expression is fully acknowledged. Slapping tradition inside out, female artists are learning to trust their own voices, but they're still struggling to be heard.

I decided to write this book because I was curious to know how the women busy tearing up rock culture felt about their position. As a journalist, I was only too familiar with the inadequacies of the media and the music business and I felt it was time for these women to speak for themselves. I wasn't surprised to discover that most of the artists I approached for interviews agreed. While some refused on the grounds of not wishing to be part of an all-women publication, and others were committed to finishing albums or writing material, most were glad of the chance to share their experiences and express their feelings.

Naturally I tailored my questions to particular topics for different artists, but there were some general themes which I wanted to explore with everyone. Each woman's background, family life, childhood and teenage years were, I believed, important in demystifying the notions surrounding them. Many turned out to have had difficult early lives, and have been forced to find inner resources to deal with their experiences. Some still have not found peace. But these experiences— abuse, rape, sexual guilt, eating disorders, self-hatred—are by no means rare; they are, unfortunately, part of women's lives the Western world over. Musicians, being all too human, are as likely to have undergone these kinds of horrors as any woman, and while nobody is making a deal out of their pain by discussing what has happened to them, whether in the light of their songs or not, each artist is helping to tear down the walls of silence, and in some cases taboo, by saying, 'Look, my life is flawed too. I'm not a victim, but neither am I a glossy, enviable untouchable!' In a world where perfect images are acquiring more value every day, such communication is crucial in shaping female culture.

I also wanted to unravel the question of a female musical vocabulary. Is there one? Do women play rock music like women, or is gender irrelevant? Most women agreed that they approached their guitar playing and songwriting in a different way to the traditional ones which have been established by male musicians. While men often seek validation of their masculinity through playing rock music, women are more likely to be challenging accepted ideas of femininity by crashing headlong into an area which has long been deemed unacceptable for nice girls.

Rock music provides women with a chance to break out of their social order, to wallow in a passionately sexual chaos of their own making, to blow up the law and roam through spaces where femininity has been throttled. Even male bands experimenting with bisexual imagery are not this free. Generally bogged down by narcissism or some such self-referential reassurance, they look to themselves in a way that women, who journey into the unknown, do not.

Lyrics too are important, because this is where artists forge their own verbal language. Women, whose very bodies have been made unfamiliar and therefore inhibitive by social forces and tradition, can realise their own powers through writing, especially in a lyric structure, where meaning can be twisted and stretched, where context is flexible and the potential of imagery endless. As Sonic Youth's Kim Gordon has pointed out, personality plays a crucial part in self-expression, and while many critics seem to forget or ignore this, it obviously explains why some women choose to plunge headlong into issues, why some opt for metaphors and storytelling and why others deal with the political through the personal.

The final common theme I wanted to examine was image. Simply by talking about their lives the women in this book revealed a great deal about how they saw themselves, so questions regarding self-image weren't always pertinent, but the topic of public image aroused unanimous disapproval and in most cases sheer anger. Every single woman I spoke with dismissed her media depictions as prejudiced, insulting, even damaging.

It seems that beneath the male gaze, female flesh and blood disappears, making way for dizzy shapes which bear no relation to the bodies on which they are based. Ancient myths of temptresses and ice queens are reactivated—Lilith, Pandora and time and again Medusa—and real female power is banished to the realm of fairy tale, where it is rendered harmless. Even when a woman is painted in 'human' terms, she still inspires freakish exaggeration and gets lost beneath piles of unreasonable embellishments.

Needless to say, instead of steely sex goddesses, harpy-like aggressors, dippy hippies and fragile little princesses sitting atop pedestals, I found all of my interviewees to be strong, interesting and talented people who were no more mysterious, unapproachable, mad or beautiful than most of my female friends.

Similarly, the women I spoke to did not exist as mere embodiments of their music. Kat Bjelland Gray, infamous for her bone-shattering, nerve-flailing noise forays with Babes in Toyland, was no more the psychotic Violet Elizabeth than Belly's Tanya Donelly was the fey, fragile, tiny, sugar-sweet doll, so often associated with her shimmering pop sensibilities.

Women are expected to personify their music in a way that men are not. Suede's Brett Anderson is thought of as interesting and sensitive rather than self-obsessed and foppish, because he is treated as a person and not a mere extension of his music. If he was seen staggering around a nightclub, no one would bat an eyelid. On the other hand, when Lush's Miki and Emma have been caught after a few beers on a Saturday night, they've been criticised for being 'laddish', instead of behaving like the good little girls behind those angel voices, while Lesley Rankine, much to her disgust, has been accused of wanting to be a man, because of her openly aggressive attitude on stage.

Of course an artist's creation is intrinsically connected to her inner core, in some cases it mixes with her very lifeblood, but this does not mean that it moulds her identity singlehandedly. Women songwriters are not rattling vessels relying solely on their art for licence to live. Songs are like concentrated fragments of emotion, character or time, they do not tell the whole story.

As Susan Faludi so eloquently illustrated with her ground-breaking analysis of the 'Undeclared War Against Women', *Backlash*, censorship of female expression, character, behaviour and culture in general is rife in the West, despite and often because of feminist advances. Within rock, the self-proclaimed rule-breaking pocket of popular culture, this censorship takes on more than a hint of irony. Sex cops police female expression, on and off stage, in song and in speech, while purporting to wield alternative ideologies. If it weren't so frustrating, it might be funny. But unfortunately, Faludi's analogy of the backlash spiral which turns women back just as they are nearing their goals rings ominously true for female musicians. Reading Sheryl Garrett and Sue Steward's lively study of women's lives in pop, *Signed, Sealed and Delivered*, from ten years ago, makes this painfully clear. Their analysis may be a decade old, but it's as valid now as it was then.

In writing this book I have tried to scrub away some of the pan-stick clogging up the formidable flow of female expression through rock music. By letting the artists speak for themselves, I hope I have handed them a chance to rectify some of the unfairness they've suffered, and also I hope that simply by collaborating with them in placing their personal histories on paper, I have helped to document a crucial time in the female history of rock for the sake of popular culture as a whole. I am all too aware of the dangers involved in embarking on a women-only project, but I am even more aware of the problems female artists still encounter and I strongly feel that discussion—whether it involves uncovering a buried history, analysing the current situation, or speaking directly to the artists themselves—is crucial if women are ever going to be accepted, appreciated and understood.

Writing about female activity in any art form, or in any aspect of life, does not have to be gratuitous or undermining, and in this book I have tried to focus on the celebration of individuals more than anything. I do not believe I have reinforced the notion of a genre of 'women-in-rock', as the very idea appals me, and I have not compared any of the women featured with each other, as to do so would be utterly absurd and completely pointless.

In choosing the women for this book, I relied partly on instinct and partly on taste. It was never to be a purely objective exercise, and to pretend otherwise would be dishonest. I feel passionate about all of these women and I see no reason, as a writer, to apologise for being emotional about my subject. But I did think about each woman's value and importance in the scheme of rock culture, and I backed up my emotional instincts with legitimate reason when I came to making decisions about who to approach. I wanted to concentrate on a wide selection of currently active artists, whose work is shaping rock culture now, to show how many ways women can take power through expression, how different these women's personalities are and how varied their agendas.

Shakespears Sister's Siobhan Fahey has used the more superficial format of pop to comment on the darker side of female emotion, and strangled the tools of glamour into something truly deranged, Echobelly's Sonya Madan confronts the strict female traditions of Asian culture lyrically and visually, Lush's Miki and Emma deal with the political on a very personal level, while Sonic Youth's Kim Gordon is making guitar rock accessible to women and questioning the idea of the fantastic rock image.

All of the women featured in this book are reclaiming a mode of expression continually denied to them, and using it to such great effect that it must surely be simply a matter of time before the representation of female rock culture catches up. It is on the brink of a shakedown, but I believe that there will be much more discussion of it by fierce women writers before its distortions are straightened out.

As the French professor, Helen Cixous, says, women have everything to write about their sexuality, about their femininity and about their becoming erotic. Now, using the language of rock music, that is exactly what women are doing.

LIZ EVANS
London
March 1994

All of the interviews in this book were conducted between June 1993 and March 1994.

Tori Amos

'*The* only place where I've never felt guilty or shameful is when I've been playing. It's the only place where I've felt in touch with my sexuality and my spirituality and my emotions, and never, ever anywhere else.'

Tori Amos

Introduction

▼

Tori Amos blew her first shivers down the spine of an unsuspecting public in 1992 when her debut solo album, *Little Earthquakes* was released. Her unnerving ability to pinpoint emotional nuances untied a well-concealed knot of female experience, while her shameless honesty and intricate powers of articulation illuminated cloudy depths of feeling. She was recognised as a genius, *Little Earthquakes* sold over a million copies worldwide, but her sanity was about to be judged.

Born in North Carolina in 1963, the then Myra Ellen Amos grew up with the pressures of a highly strict religion. Her father, Eddie, and his parents were all ministers of the Church of God, a by-product of Methodism, while her mother was part Cherokee Native American. Able to play the piano before she could talk, Amos was a child prodigy and at the age of five was enrolled at Baltimore's prestigious Peabody Institute for gifted children.

Until she was 21 Amos went to church four times a week, teaching the children's choir and quietly resenting Jesus' demands on her life. Eventually she fled to Los Angeles, reinvented herself with a new name (after a tree), big hair and plastic snakeskin pants, threw herself passionately into the city's decadent rock-'n'roll scene of the mid-eighties and released a record *Y Kant Tori*

Read? which flopped bigtime.

After being mocked as a bimbo by the American music trade paper *Billboard* and laughed at in local restaurants, Amos recoiled from the hard world of Hollywood show business and had something of a nervous breakdown. She'd also suffered a vicious sexual attack in the back of a car and lost touch with the sexuality which had only recently shaken off the guilt of a Methodist childhood.

The result of all this was *Little Earthquakes*, a collection of songs through which Amos came to terms with her past. The a capella 'Me And A Gun' dealt with the rape of five years before, while the rest explored the themes of guilt, God and sexuality which had governed Amos' life.

Although they'd handed her a contract, Amos' American record label were unable to cope with a girl and her piano, so they sent her to London where she finally realised her lifetime ambition to make real music, but while many applauded her provocative openness, others were baffled into reaching for the nearest convenient trough in which to pitch her. Her acuteness was simply too much for some and too often she was stripped of her individual agenda, tossed in with a string of female singer-songwriters including everyone from Kate Bush to Patti Smith and, worst of all, was said to be mad.

Rock has always celebrated the more romantic side of insanity, encouraging its quirky eccentrics in their agonising struggles to create. Outcasts who find solace in the delirium of their art are more than welcome in the world of popular entertainment, but usually only if they're male. Female artists who function left of centre are often treated with scorn, ridicule and ignorance. Amos was no exception.

Even when her second album, *Under The Pink,* was released in 1994, flying straight into the British charts at number one, Amos was still being touted as some kind of 'kooky babe'. Although this time nobody went so far as to suggest that her only selling point was 'mental decrepitude', Amos' 'fruitcake' qualities were still highlighted at the expense of her extraordinary talent.

Amos isn't interested in being 'normal' although she has been hurt by the unkindness of certain factions of the media. Her main concern is to make music and if her expressions don't tumble out in neat orderly rows, well, so what?

While there is nothing particularly neat and orderly about Tori Amos, there is certainly nothing decrepit about her mentally or otherwise. In coming to terms with her repressive religious childhood, the sexual guilt it induced, a brutal attack, and more recently the hurt of broken female friendships and the ways in which women betray each other, Amos has developed a highly intuitive emotional vocabulary and bravely explores hitherto silent corridors of her own and many other women's inner lives. To call this a sign of madness is, in itself, mad.

Tori Amos

*M*y relationships with my family were very different when I was a child, because it was a very disciplined Methodist household. My father was reared in the Church of God, and he was a very conservative, Victorian kind of man. My grandmother, on his side, believed that all girls should be virgins, and that if you didn't come that way to your husband you were not one of God's children and you'd go to hell. She tried to pin that on me—good thing she died before I was a teenager! I was 13 when she died but the damage was done. I don't have ill feelings, but I've had to work through a lot of the things I took on then.

Now, who's to say what I'd be writing about if I didn't have my background? Yet at the same time, this is only a taste of what the church has done for thousands of years. Our whole Goddess culture has been destroyed, and what has the female deity role model become? The Virgin Mary! And for our Goddess, who is our mother of fertility and passion, to be a virgin—well, what do we have to live up to? From the starting block, from get-go, we're minus ten! The idea of virginity has so affected us. And it's not just Christianity, it's all over the planet.

I've written a song called 'God' [single released in America, January 1994] about patriarchal religion, and how it's just fucked the whole thing up. Basically I say to Him, 'You know, you need a babe and I've got nothing to do Tuesday and Thursday this week!' It's unacceptable in how it's affected people. And it isn't just women who've been affected. Men have had to cut out a whole part of themselves too, which is why we have to deal with all that shit from our boyfriends! Men and women are going to have to recognise the female energy that we've cut out.

'Cornflake Girl' [single released in Britain, January 1994] deals with it too. There's a book by Alice Walker called *Possessing the Secret of Joy*, and it's about mothers taking their daughters to the butcher to have their genitalia removed. That's what the song is about too. It's like cutting a penis off. Now if we lined all the boys up and cut their penises off, I don't think it would be lunch as usual! I think they'd have something to say about it, and yet the mothers are the ones that take the daughters to do this! Obviously the whole society is involved, but when is a generation of women going to rise up, not to fight, not to war, but to honour themselves and each other?

I think the time of the Goddess is coming. I know I have to stop all the shit I took on as a child in my life, because I don't want to pass it down to other men and women. So I've tried to become my own parent, shall we say, and retrain some of those patterns.

I had good memories of who I was before I was five, and then I became everybody else's idea of who I was. Before I was five I was at the piano most of the time, and kind of oblivious to stuff. I mean, I could sense things but I wasn't aware of shame or anything. I distinctly remember having no inhibitions creatively at that age. I think we all remember if we look back. And then I just started to get used to different people's critiques of my being and I let it influence me. It's so difficult to be critical of children because they need to discover themselves. We're always telling them—'No, the tree has green leaves!'

Maybe I've reacted so intensely because it's taken me 25 years to get back to the freedom that I had when I was that age, and I've had to work backwards to get it. The whole idea was for me to be a concert pianist and it didn't happen. It wasn't going to happen because I wanted to compose my own songs, I always knew that. And after a year, it wasn't fun at the Peabody Institute, where I was sent to train at the weekends, because I was disappointing everybody and I felt that I was. It was like 'Oh the girl that has so much talent can't do this and can't do that', and they'd put money on my wrists to get me playing right. I'd be wanting to know when we were going to make up fun songs, but nobody was interested in that. It was all about developing a technique and becoming competitive.

By the time I was 8, I kind of knew what was going on. I didn't really make any friends there, but there was this older boy who kind of looked like Jimi Hendrix who I had a crush on. I wrote a song for him, but he left and I never saw him again. People would come and go and I was there for years. I'd take classes all day Saturday, and then during the week I went back home and went to normal school, so I lived a dual life. It was kind of freaky.

Sometimes I wonder if it would have made more sense if I'd done one or the other. At normal school I had to sit in the corner because they felt I disturbed the class. I used to get bored and talk to my neighbours. They put me in the back, and it was weird—I felt like an idiot! They thought I could do one thing and nothing else, because I was going to the Peabody, and maybe it was true! It's all I did, it's all I do, it's all I've ever done!

As a Methodist, I remember going to church four times a week, and I did that until I was 21. I was teaching the children's choir and I used to get really pissed off that my life was so dictated by when this Jesus guy was born and when he was dying every year. I felt really resentful that I couldn't get on with my own life, because I was so busy with his. Of course the real energy of Jesus had nothing to do with it. When I tune into the real energy of it, I just see a really evolved master teacher who was used to giving people control. But at the time I felt subjected to it, and made to feel guilty when I didn't want to be a part of it, because this was our faith and this was what we believed in. There would be prayer meetings at our house, and I'd think 'How do I escape this?' My song 'Icicle' has a lot to do with it. It's about how this girl masturbates just to survive!

The best thing that happened at that time was when I started working in gay bars at the age of 13. The funny thing is my father used to chaperone me! I think he came to realise that you either supported your kid or you lost them, and a lot of my friends were getting pregnant. A lot of them had had abortions by the time they were 14.

I had a boyfriend but it was very hard for him. I couldn't make it work and that frustrated me. Now I have freedom in my life and I can do what I want, I don't think about it so much except maybe when I'm writing something like 'Icicle'.

The strangest thing was that those church people had the best intentions. But it was never about individuality, and so I could never believe the fundamental beliefs.

Eventually I left, and I moved to Los Angeles when I was 21. I felt like a kid in a candy shop. I'd be driving down the road and—Mmmm! There was a guy and Mmmm! There was a guy!—And I was free on Sundays! And it was 1985 right? That was the time! It was a great time, a very happy, perky time in LA. Everyone you met was in a band. I was playing piano bar to pay the rent and I lived in East Hollywood, below Mann's Chinese Theatre. A whole bunch of musicians lived there, near Beechwood, and it was very easy going, because we were all in the same boat, and there was a camaraderie which is something I was looking for at the time, instead of competition which just doesn't help anybody.

So I was hanging out with friends who were in bands, and partying without feeling too guilty, although I carried a bit of it with me. But to be honest, there are things I'm grateful I didn't do. Like sleep with two bisexual models at the same time! They were so gorgeous and I wanted to be the baloney in between the wholewheat bread but I'm kind of thankful now that I didn't, because that's when so much of the AIDS thing was running rampant there, and I'm glad that I sometimes, sometimes practised caution. Sometimes. Enough.

It was so hedonistic, and it's so nice to know I was there in the decadence. It was healing for me. It was like being baptised, being in Sodom and Gomorrah! I was there with my little chopsticks going 'Isn't anybody hungry?' Really happy, pouring tea and stuff.

I did refuse to look at a lot of stuff in my life, though. I closed the door on everything I didn't want to look at. Instead of pouring how I really felt into my music, I dressed a certain way and became part of a culture. I was beginning to reclaim a part of myself, I just had to do it through clothes first before I was willing to talk about it. I'd put on my plastic snakepants and they'd feel so good! There was a sense of sexual power feeling them next to my skin, especially when I knew what all those ladies in the soprano section of the church choir were doing!

Being a rock chick like that is so *DC Comics*, so *Rocky Horror Picture Show* and eight or nine years ago we just didn't think about it. All my girlfriends had white hair pumped up with Aqua Net. We were differentiating ourselves from the Reagan generation I guess, we'd been fucked over by the 1960s children so we thought fuck them! You know? Peace my ass! Give me my stiletto boots and if that motherfucker crosses me I'm going to blow his fucking head off! It was all very hard—with a sense of humour.

I joined a band around that time and we made a record called *Y Kant Tori Read?* But by the time it came out, the band had broken up. We just couldn't get along, so we went our separate ways, and now the drummer is in Guns N' Roses. Actually the guitar player played on my second solo album. Looking at it objectively, the record wasn't that good. As a band we were better. But hey, I did that record. I don't place blame, and hey, I chose to look like that too. I chose to not speak about things, I chose to not stick up for the band when the heat got rough and I chose to turn it over to more male presences. And so the band split up and the record came out and they called me a bimbo in *Billboard* magazine and people would laugh at me in restaurants in LA. And I think the laughter is what really got to me, because you have to remember where I came from. These people who were laughing at me were pissing on themselves when I could play concertos.

It took me a minute to ask myself why I was making music—for what reason? I wanted to be successful for my father because I never got the doctorate in music, which is what he wanted me to do. But I wanted to do it on my own terms and I fell on my face. It was the biggest gift though, because then I started to see pretty much everything for what it was in the whole music world. And that's when I nearly had a nervous breakdown. I was on the kitchen floor for so long I could count over a thousand tiles.

But I really had to reclaim myself. I had untraditional therapy which I don't really want to define and I started to write *Little Earthquakes*. I got a keyboard in my apartment, and although I hadn't played in years, my chops were up from working in piano bars.

And I started to write for the sole reason of expression, which is what I did when I was four. So that's why it took me 20 years to get back to that place. It was strange at first, but it was like a turtle going back into water again. It felt good, I wasn't doing it for anyone else—not to get out of the church, not for boys to like me, not for dad to think I was OK. Just to do it, just to express things. If it's not an expression, why bother?

Little Earthquakes was the acknowledgment of things I hadn't looked at for 15 years. I'd been sexually attacked in Los Angeles and I hadn't dealt with that for five years either. When it was released, a lot of people who'd listened to it or seen my shows told me they'd had similar experiences to the ones I was expressing. It was like sitting round a table at a party where everyone feels better for getting stuff off their chests! But guess what? Soon the party's over and you have to go home and wake up and ask yourself—'How am I not going to be a victim anymore? How am I going to wake up and not feel guilty that I want passion in my life?' When you combine sex and guilt with Christianity, it's insane!

I was shocked by how many women I met who'd had experiences where they were raped or were about ready to be killed though. And you'd be surprised how many women feel responsible when they don't even know their attackers. I felt responsible when it happened to me.

My attack was very involved—everybody's is very involved. I'm still having to get over what my role was in it, and deal with my hatred towards my attacker and towards myself, because I took on his hatred of me. He hated women and I just took on that hatred. The hardest thing for me to get over is that I really thought it was over. He had said how he was going to murder me and I really thought that was it. And then there's the fear and degradation of it all.

Afterwards I started to think, well it's one thing to talk about it, but it's another to really put life back into life again. To get those pictures out of my mind when I'm intimate with a man. I'm just having to discipline myself, and say 'Well, hey! This is not the same thing period. Period!' And it takes so much will, because if you let your mind dwell on how you feel, it can be very addictive. I think I have at times. And I don't want that anymore.

Now I realise I do have a choice with my sexual role and sexuality has so much more to do with things other than penises and vaginas. It has to do with my connection to the universe and the earth and my whole being, and if I want to share that with another human being, then I can. But my sexuality doesn't stem from needing somebody else to give that to me. I have to give it to myself. Once I start to do that then that violent attack stops being the thing that's taken everything away from me.

So I'm going to work through it. Abuse is abuse and when you're terrorised you're terrorised and sometimes you cut out parts of yourself to survive. I tried to cut out parts of myself before he did and I didn't claim them back. I also cut out parts of myself to survive the Christian upbringing, because it's easier if you numb those parts a little bit, put the ice on them. I don't know, it's your last little bit of power–that you do it before someone else does it. So now what I've had to do is light up some matches and go be a little pyro, and warm up those parts again. And I wrote my second album, *Under The Pink*, while I was doing that, so really it's the next step of applying what I was acknowledging with the first record.

I think I was still really scared after *Little Earthquakes* though. I still had to sort other things out sexually. I played 250 cities with this last record, and a lot of women were offended by the way I played piano, and that did something to shake me out of my fear because I had to say 'Hang on a minute, why am I doing this?' I think when you're confronted by people it wakes you up a little bit, so that you do have to question yourself.

These women were supposedly left-wing feminists, saying they were really offended by the way I was playing because I was making myself an object. But I didn't see myself as an object, this was how I felt good playing. And I still do. Not only do I support myself physically, but it is a very passionate thing. Again, it's about sexuality beyond the penis and vagina, so if anyone wants to see it as a shot in *Penthouse*, then that's their concept, and if I see it as my expression of my sexuality, then that's what it is for me. It's really between me, my piano, the earth and my soul, and how I'm just kind of in this line of energy that's moving down from the top, through me, into the earth.

Some of these feminists become fascists, because they're saying if I don't do certain things that they deem appropriate then I'm not a strong independent woman. Bullshit! Whether it's the concerned mothers of America or the left-wing feminists who have to try and censor things and try and attack you, to me it's fascist either way. My whole thing is knock yourself out, do whatever feels good, and if you cross my boundaries where you hurt me or mine then I'll draw my line and naturally stand up for what I believe in. But if you want to do this in your life and it affects you, who am I to say? I don't believe in dictating to people.

Being betrayed by another woman, I think, cuts the deepest. That point, when another woman can't come through for you, especially when you're friends, is so much more painful than anything guys dole out. And guys shouldn't take this wrong, but we expect them to not come through sometimes, or betray us, even if it's not intentional. I can't justify it when women betray me, because I can't think,

'Well, he just wanted to go to the ballgame, so of course he got a little confused!' As women we're very aware of what each of us has to go through, so when one of us denies that, and doesn't take responsibility for our part in a relationship, it's really painful.

I've always had this idea about the sisterhood, and it's not about alienating men, it's just about honouring other women, and being more accepting of each other because of what we've been through. But I've found more viciousness from women than men, because men aren't really vicious. They can be ignorant and insensitive, and they sometimes lose control, because it's in their genes and they've done it for thousands of years. But this sisterhood concept that I wanted to look at while I was growing up, and kept wanting to turn to, never materialised. Friends never fulfilled the idea, and the older I've got, the colder the water that's been poured on my head.

You know how manipulative women can be, we can just not say things, which can be very hurtful. You know if you get a job and your friend doesn't acknowledge you or congratulate you or support you in any way, but just starts saying 'Be careful, be careful' as if maybe you're not capable of handling it. So I am beginning to pull women into my life who are really trying to take responsibility for their part in the relationship. It's a recent thing, because I'm taking more responsibility in what I'm dumping.

I've also had to deal with my violence, because sometimes the hurt of being betrayed is so great, it can make me feel very violent. Although I can hold my own in a rough moment, and I can actually feel quite good—like Sven the Viking!—I don't really want to live with that kind of energy. I'd rather just say 'Hey, why am I letting this ruin my week, my day, my month? Maybe we just shouldn't hang out anymore.'

Women who cut themselves off from their emotions so that they can survive in this world of male dominance and logic have a real problem with any kind of emotional expression, because they learn to be analytical and in control. I'm not interested in that because if somebody's moved by something, and they want to get loud about it, that's fine. A lot of people are emotionally cut off from what they're talking about, and when it's a woman it can really hurt sometimes when you're trying to have a conversation, and she says something a guy could say. Like 'Oh, you must be having your period!'

When I'm really upset or fucked up or angry about something, it's not because of my father or because I haven't been laid recently, it's because I'm very fucked off about the issue in hand. In music, a lot of women get approached on an emotional plane, and that's when they cut themselves off. It's very difficult sometimes because when you're creative you are trying to break patterns and become an individual, and often it's not even encouraged by your own camp.

I don't want to be normal, because normal is about the status quo, which I don't want to be a part of. I've never read that people buy my records because I'm kooky though. A lot of the time that stuff just makes good reading. People play games when they've got you under the microscope, and when they don't understand something I say, or an experience that I've talked about, they jump on it and try and make it look silly or insane. I don't know where they come from. I just try and be forthright and give interesting answers. I guess some of the things I've read about me I haven't recognised, but being true to your music is not about press cuttings.

I mean I've done music since before I could talk, and that's why when some music head gives me an opinion, I say 'Look, I don't know how this works, but if it didn't I couldn't sit here and listen to it, I'd be sick, I couldn't keep my spaghetti down!' And keeping my spaghetti down is the test. I'm physically involved with it. And I'm pretty harsh, I'm pretty ruthless which is why I can never play the real difficult piano things twice. I have to make them up every time. It doesn't come from my head, it comes from my stomach, and depends on the moment, and what's happened during the day and how long I pause at that second, and if I hit with my left hand and the rhythm changes—I couldn't get that back! It's a completely physical thing for me, the whole kundalini is very much involved. And you know what, the only place where I've never felt guilty or shameful is when I've been playing. It's the only place where I've felt in touch with my sexuality and my spirituality and my emotions, and never, ever, ever anywhere else. So my life is a bit tricky because when I'm not playing, I'm just trying to walk down the street!

I have always cut out everything, except when I played. When you feel bad about being a girl and you have thoughts about masturbating and thoughts about doing it with boys—I mean I wanted to do it with Robert Plant so bad!—and you're eight or nine, it's rough. You don't know what 'doing it' is, but you want to do it! And you kind of know that 'it's' the thing that Grandma's been talking about. The last thing you want to do is lose respect from your father, but when you're that age, you're starting to be a pest. You're not so cute, you're starting to develop things but you're not old enough to do anything with them, and it's really hard. But playing was where I had freedom, and even today that's where I have the most freedom.

I think I'd like to get to a place in my life where I'm not destroyed by ugly situations and I won't take them personally. And I can still grow. And maybe if I've done something which has been misunderstood I can say 'Ok, I did that' and I won't have to go away feeling like I'll never make that mistake again. Because I will!

I do tend to work things out in my songs and usually something I've been hiding comes out—a certain feeling—and it's freeing, it's painful and it's liberating. And I really can't walk around and be crippled for the rest of my life. It's false to think that musicians and artists have to suffer for their work. It's a myth. I want to hear from someone who's fulfilled because I want to be in that place where we're not bumbling around anymore.

I think I could lighten up a little more, give it a rest at the dinner table and enjoy the moment a little more because I do believe in hope for anything. If we're tied to the stake and it's over for us, there's still that possibility that Mary Poppins' sister—the one who was making out in the cinema with the runs in her hose—just might come hopping down the lane at that time and help us out. And once the match is struck and we're going, I'm still hanging onto that thought—'God damn, she was supposed to come!' And if we have to do it all again, I still think she might.

Credentials

Signed to: East West Records
Managed by: Arthur Spivak
Select discography: *Little Earthquakes* LP (1992)
                        Under The Pink LP (1994)

Emma Anderson

'*Of* course I'm a feminist, but when it comes to music ... you can't do it by saying, "I'm a woman! I'm a woman!" You've just got to get on with it.'

Miki Berenyi

'*I* think it takes more guts for a woman to write a song where she admits that she finds other women a threat, than it does for her to sham it and say "Oh, I love all other women" because nobody loves everybody. It's a lie.'

Emma Anderson and Miki Berenyi

Introduction

Together with their band Lush, Miki Berenyi and Emma Anderson have found their way into a world of immaculately-honed images and preened personas without so much as a nod to contrived cool. Backed by a male rhythm section, the two songwriters, vocalists and guitarists have kept clear of the frontgirl traps and focused on presenting themselves as an integral part of a four-piece band, resisting the attempts of the music industry to turn them into little princesses. Their beautifully dreamy soundscapes have provoked criticisms of political apathy, but as Berenyi and Anderson point out, sloganeering hasn't been their method since they were a college band clumsily protesting against page three girls. These days they prefer to deal with the political on a personal level, and while this approach may prove too subtle for male journalists demanding easily identifiable party lines, it holds much more relevance for most women.

Berenyi and Anderson met at school, where they recognised a mutual 'outsider' quality in each other. They sought solace from the material and sexual competitiveness of their classmates in music and often took in four or five gigs a week. When they graduated to their respective colleges, they began playing guitar; Berenyi joined The Bugs and Anderson The Rover Girls, until finally they decided to pool their efforts and take the risk of forming their own unit, Lush. Meriel Barham, now with the Pale Saints, was their original vocalist, but quit early on because of boyfriend trouble, leaving Berenyi to reluctantly take over after a string of hapless auditions for a replacement. Despite their lack of confidence and experience, Lush quickly grabbed the attention of the music press, and managed to secure a record deal in 1989 with 4AD, the Cocteau Twins' label. After recording a handful of singles which were compiled as *Gala* and an album *Spooky*, Lush replaced their first bassist, Steve Rippon, with Phil King and have recently released their third album, *Split*.

Sharing the songwriting, Berenyi and Anderson never collaborate, working apart to accommodate their very different methods. Berenyi tends to write specifically about people or situations, while Anderson has an abstract, visual, almost poetic approach, although sonically they both deal in swirling guitar storms and delicate melodies.

Berenyi's directness typifies her outspokenness on feminist issues and her scathing 'unpolitically-correct' views on sugar-candied pop kittens have landed her in trouble with the same journalists who condemn Lush's music for not being militant enough. Anderson is more understated about things, preferring to make changes through her example alone, although she has been equally outraged by the injustices thrown at Lush as Berenyi. Injustices which have included accusations that the two women were controlled and manipulated by an army of male record producers and managers, that they probably hadn't even played on their own records and that they weren't 'angry' enough compared to Babes in Toyland and Hole—all categorical proof that women who make and play music are still subject to absurd comparisons, spiteful judgements and childish prejudice.

Steadfastly ignoring their detractors, Berenyi and Anderson have continued to project themselves through their music and the image machinery of rock with as little fuss as possible. They find the anonymity of bland glamour distasteful and boring, so they don't bother with it, nor do they make a point of dressing down to please the radicals. They haven't souped up their melodies to satisfy the ears of angst-hungry listeners because they have never raged loudly and they're not about to start now simply because other women choose to express themselves in that way. And they haven't stunted their perfectly ordinary pub-going, nightclubbing activities to fit in with the ethereal fantasies conjured up by their heavenly sound, despite being implicated in gossip columns every time they appear at a party. They're just themselves and while this isn't as comfortable yet as it ought to be for women in the public eye, Lush are proving that it is far from impossible.

Emma Anderson

In Her Own Words

I was an only child and my parents were quite old when they had me. My mum was 37 and my dad was 48. I suppose I had quite a privileged upbringing. They were very middle class so I went to private schools but I rebelled against everything. Everything. Every single thing, from when I was really quite young.

I had a bit of a difficult relationship with my parents, I don't want to slag them off but it was hard. I think my mother had ideas above her station. She could only judge me by what she'd done, but she wanted me to be a debutante or something, even though it was completely out of date. She'd say things like 'Oh when you get married we'll have your picture in the *Tatler*.' My dad was in the army so she wanted me to marry someone in the army. And she had all these ideas for me about dressing me up in pretty little frocks!

One thing about them, though, they were always totally in love, there was never any unhappiness between them at all. They never argued. I think my mum's upbringing was very much to do with her being a girl, so that was her lot. She went to a private school but she didn't have a very good education. She had a brother and he had a job, but she wasn't allowed to have one. The only way she could leave home was to get married so she married this bloke – whom she later divorced – when she was 19, and he treated her really badly. And I think she found it a bit difficult to understand me growing up in the 1980s and dyeing my hair, and getting into music, it was so alien to her, and not what she wanted me to do.

From when I was 2 until I was 14, we lived in this old boys' army club, where retired army blokes came for a drink with their friends. It was just off Piccadilly in Half Moon Street. It was a bit dodgy, people used to come in so they could have a free drink and my mother was entertaining the whole time, so I always had to be in my bedroom or out with friends. And my father always had to be there so we never had holidays. Again if I had a holiday, I'd go with friends. Being tied so much to that place was really what led to my dad's first heart attack. He died two years ago.

In some ways living there was quite interesting though, because as you can imagine lots of things went on there and there were all these interesting characters around. But it was a strange upbringing for a kid and I think they felt a bit guilty. So they were never stingy with me and they always let me out with my friends and I never had to be in at a certain time. They gave me pocket money and bought me a guitar. I guess the whole thing was a bit double-edged.

The thing that was really strange about my parents was that they thought education was really unimportant and I rebelled because I wanted to do my exams. They wanted me to do a domestic science course at 16, and I got myself into college to do 'A' levels and they said 'You're not going!' And I said 'Well I'm not going to do domestic science, I'm not signing the form!' It was so weird!

They'd sent me to all these private schools, hoping I'd meet the right people, and who do I meet? Miki! A lot of those schools were full of people who had so much money that I couldn't keep up with them. I had to leave my first boarding school because my parents couldn't afford it, so they took me away in the middle of my

'O' levels. I went to Queens School which is where I met Miki. There was me in my C&A clothes and Marks and Spencer shoes in the middle of all these very moneyed Jewish girls. I'm not being racist at all, but their wealth was a cultural thing. They all had huge houses and expensive clothes and big cars, and they had their own scene. Probably the reason why me and Miki originally hung together was because we didn't have Gucci shoes! I was just the kid at the back and no, my family didn't have a car!

My mum never liked Miki. I think she thought Miki was a bad influence on me, which wasn't true at all. I think I'd always been attracted to some form of alternative thinking. I'd first got into music when I was about eight and I was really into The Beatles, but I was starved of music when I was at home because my parents didn't have a record player or anything. I used to watch *Top Of The Pops* until eventually I got a record player.

During the fourth year at boarding school we were allowed out to town once a week and we were allowed to listen to the radio and so I started to buy music magazines. The weird thing was I could only listen to the Top 40 at the time, but I started getting into the Teardrop Explodes and The Undertones, while everyone else was getting into Elton John, and anything else their big brothers and sisters were listening to. So I was totally on my own. All the others were cutting up fashion magazines and putting up the pictures on their walls, and I was just not into that.

I suppose when you're that age, in your early teens, you start becoming interested in the way you dress, but I was a bit of a frump and I never fitted in with that. I had loads of friends so I wasn't a square or anything, but I thought what they were doing was really conservative. I didn't think it was very big to be into make up and smoking and boys, maybe because my mother had been, and I wanted to be a bit more of a tomboy and buy records. I probably couldn't impress boys at that age even if I'd wanted to because I was fat and they wouldn't have looked twice at me!

I was such a late starter with men. Having been to boarding school I never met any until I started going to gigs with Miki. At Queens all the girls would be talking about who'd finger-fucked them at the University College Hospital ball, while we were going to see bands and reading the music papers out to each other. Everyone thought we were mad. We had these horrible old army coats and we started writing band names on them and on our desks and pencil cases! I think we took refuge in music actually. We were probably the only ones in the school into it. But even Miki was going out with boys before me. I was the fat friend living in Piccadilly and I'd been to girls' schools all my life.

The funny thing was, before I went to boarding school I was as thin as a rake, the smallest thing in the class. Then I went to that school and all the food was starchy and we did a lot of sport so I ate a lot. I didn't really think about being fat until I started going out to see bands. I actually went on a diet and lost a stone, but I put it back on. Then later I lost a load of weight when I split up with one of my boyfriends. I was really unhappy but I never put the weight back on! And about three years ago I was going through a really bad emotional time with this bloke, and I was dieting again. It was during a period of time when we were writing songs for *Spooky*, our second album, and I couldn't write a thing. This time round, while I've been writing for the third album, I've been eating whenever I've been hungry and it's been so much easier. Why did I ever worry about it? I was just miserable and what's the point of being miserable? And I lost so much weight that I actually got to the point where I looked pretty awful. My face was all sunken and my tits went all saggy and it was really unattractive. I looked old. I went to under eight stone on that last diet and one day I looked in the mirror and I thought, well, this is really stupid. I thought fuck it, and just left it. I mean obviously if you're seriously obese it's different, but I think we all suffer from this dieting mentality and it's such a distracting thing. It's all to do with your self-perception really.

Anyway, luckily, when I was 14 I was much more bothered about going to gigs than impressing boys. Me and Miki got into bands in a very juvenile teeny way. We liked Duran Duran and Haircut 100, but we also liked New Order and the Cocteau Twins and we used to go and see anarcho-punk bands and gothy bands. We'd go out five nights a week, and although my parents didn't really like it, they never stopped me. I think they thought it was just a phase.

My dad was probably more understanding about me and music than my mum. I think my mum would still have liked me to have done a cooking course and married a nice man and got a nice house and had babies. I get angry with her sometimes, but my parents were older, they come from such a different background. A lot of my friends' parents partook in all the things that went on in the 1960s, but my parents didn't. My mum always said feminists were cutting off their own noses! Sometimes I wonder if she's jealous of me, because she wasn't allowed to do things that I've done. When my mum first got married she said she knew she was doing the wrong thing while she was walking up the aisle. But that was the only way she could leave home. Her heyday was in the 1950s, so I can't really expect her to understand my life.

She says she likes my music, but I don't know if she does. She hates drums, she always asks me why I can't write songs without them. But she's been to see us a few times. And when we're on telly or we get a review in the *Daily Telegraph* she loves it. I think she thinks it could all fall through tomorrow, and then what would I do. I just tell her it's not that bad and that there are other people to work with. She thinks Lush is like a modelling career, you get older and you can't do it anymore!

The first female artist I remember getting into was Kate Bush, I thought she was brilliant. And I was a massive Abba fan. But when I was young I wasn't really aware of women in bands. Me and Miki were really into our teeny bands and apart from Siouxsie Sioux and Kate Bush, there weren't that many women in the Top 40. On the more alternative side, when I was about 16, there was the Cocteau Twins and Xmal Deutschland who I thought were brilliant because there were four girls and one bloke in the band and the drummer was a woman. There weren't many women playing guitar though. There were all those bands like The Slits and The Au Pairs and The Raincoats and that scene, but when you're younger you get into what's in front of you, and they weren't.

When I started 'A' levels at Paddington College I didn't do anything apart from studying, although I did have three guitar lessons! My cousin gave me a guitar, which I still write songs on, and Miki'd bought one from a friend, so we started playing Blondie and Abba songs really badly at my parents home in St Johns Wood. We used to plug into the stereo.

During my year off between 'A' levels and Ealing College, where I did my degree, I worked at the DHSS office and I bought a bass guitar. It's very easy to pick up bass. I'd meet up once a week with Miki and we'd play in my kitchen.

The week I started going to Ealing I joined this band called The Rover Girls. I'd met the others, Chris and Stuart, who are now with Silverfish, from going to gigs, and when they lost their bass player I stepped in. They just did Elvis covers, it was a joke thing really. The biggest gig we did was with The Primitives, Gaye Bykers on Acid and My Bloody Valentine at the Astoria. That was our moment of fame. And it all went downhill from there.

Miki was playing with The Bugs, but neither of us took what we were doing very seriously although I think the reason we ended up playing in our own band was because we weren't confident enough to play with anyone else. We couldn't play but we were enthusiastic. When we actually got Lush together we wanted to play sets and we realised we weren't that much worse than a lot of the other bands around.

The others in Lush were all at college together and Miki and Chris, the drummer, used to go out together so I was a bit left out at first. I probably had more ambition because of that, though, so I took more on board. I was more of a loner I suppose. I used to go to gigs on my own, and I got to know a lot of people. And I used to always book the gigs because I knew people and I used to send tapes out, and I enjoyed it. Nobody else did that at all.

After our first singer, Meriel, left it was a turning point. Meriel wasn't at all confident and she didn't like being a singer, and she had this boyfriend who was uppermost in her mind. So we parted company. I suggested to Miki that she sing, because she was a million times better than all the people we auditioned. I can't sing at all.

I definitely had a turning point in writing then. I sat down and thought about it a lot more. I never thought about expressing myself as a woman exactly, I just wanted to write better songs. It sounds boring, but I think I express myself like that anyway. Obviously the lyrics are female, there's no getting away from that, but the actual music itself is just music.

A lot of people get themselves across through aggression, and we do have some aggressive songs but it's nothing to do with needing to do that as a woman. It's just because we like the music. Of course I'm a feminist but when it comes to music it's just a case of doing it as well as possible and in that way maybe I want to make a point. Just by doing it is saying something in itself. You can't do it by saying 'I'm a woman, I'm a woman!' You've just got to get on with it.

We've been ripped apart by certain male journalists for 'having nothing to say'. But how many men in bands have got messages? It's like, if you're a woman in a band you have to talk about being feminist! You can't just sing about normal things. The Stone Roses didn't have a message did they? People are so naïve. I think really men are threatened by women doing it and they can't grab hold of it if it's not on their terms.

Lyrically, Miki's more direct than me. She writes about people who've pissed her off whereas I play with words and images a lot more. Sometimes if I hear lyrics of mine which are quite obvious, I cringe because I don't feel that way about the person anymore!

Obviously me and Miki are really quite different people. She's quite a dark person and her upbringing was very different to mine. I think I enjoy my own company a lot more than she does. She doesn't like to be alone too much. She had a really bad childhood though. I mean, I rowed with my parents but I never had anything like Miki and she's grown up and coped with it and turned it into something. A lot of people would be in an asylum if they'd been through what she has, and she isn't, she's very strong and she's learnt to deal with her past, although sometimes it rears it's head.

I'm not saying I'm particularly stable, though, because I'm not. I go through really shit periods and I can't write when I'm unhappy. Sometimes I write about emotions that I'm sure Miki doesn't feel because we have a very different experience of life and our personal lives are so different. If I'm writing something heartwrenching I always think she's thinking what a prat I am! But we rely on each other and she knows about the shit I go through, so what the hell.

I'm not really into poetry but my lyrics are quite poetic. I can't paint or draw either and it sounds really pretentious but when I write a song it has to have a good shape and a good colour. I've never really talked about this to anyone before but I thought about it the other day, and there definitely has to be a good shape to the melodies. I mean I couldn't draw these shapes, they're just in my head and they're hard to put into words as well. I just develop mental pictures of them.

I always think that I'm instinctive about songwriting, and I think with Miki it's a lot more mathematical. She'll sit down and work it all out, and I usually start with a melody in my head. I work it out and I tape it. It usually happens in really odd situations, like when I'm cleaning the toilet. There'll be this melody in my head, and I'll try and remember where it's from and it's not actually from anywhere, it's from my head. 'Deluxe' I came up with when I was making sandwiches where I worked, and I sang it all the way home on the tube and taped it when I got home!

I just can't sit there and write chords. I think if you listen to a lot of female music, it's a lot more meandering, it's not quite so mathematical. Sometimes I feel uncomfortable saying there's a female way of doing it, because men write songs like that as well. And I think some of the songs I write are really quite traditional even in the structure. I have thought about it but not to a great extent. I've never tried to cultivate a female sound, it's just something that comes naturally. I've never thought, well I'm a woman and I've got to prove myself. Obviously the issue has come up, but when we started we never thought about it. The fact that you do it is enough. You do it and you want to do it well. We never thought, oh we could be really hard done by because we're girls. We never came up against problems because we were girls. I had this conversation with one of Fuzzbox once and she said, 'God don't you get it really hard from your record company, aren't they really sexist?' And I said, 'Well, no not at all.' And she said 'Well we're on EMI and no one takes us seriously there.' And I thought, well hang on a minute you dress up in those stupid little costumes and you can't play! I'm not saying they should have worn dungarees or anything, but they were so pathetic. They had this image with loads of negligees, and I thought, well, *I* don't take you seriously!

Having said that, we were aware that if we'd signed to a major label they would definitely have wanted to glamorise me and Miki. We weren't interested in majors though. I'd been living in London and going to gigs, and we were quite aware of the way things worked.

When we started getting press it never went to our heads. We did take things quite slowly, and we played a lot. A lot of people thought we came out of nowhere but we played every fucking toilet twice. And Miki always had trouble singing in a small place because Chris plays his drums really loud, and we weren't confident at all. We had singing lessons eventually! It helps having someone behind you as well because we never had a manager or roadies or anyone in the beginning. We did it all ourselves.

The fact that we were girls was never an issue initially. It became one after we got signed and the media got involved and started taking pictures of just me or just Miki. We tried hard not to let it happen, but it did. Obviously Miki is quite unique in the way she looks and we did start the band and we write all the songs so there is that side to it, but at the same time that's where it ends. I hate seeing photos of myself anyway.

Videos are the worst though. There were a couple of things which got slightly out of control, when we were made to look really glamorous in videos.

And once we did a photo session with this fashion photographer for 4AD. We saw his portfolio and the pictures were really good, but when we got there he had this make-up artist and he wanted to do all these things to our hair. He told Miki she should shave her armpits! I had to tell them to stop. It was totally wrong. They were telling Chris to undo his shirt. It was terrible. I think we were naïve because we thought they were going to do a proper job. But a lot of people don't know anything about Lush and they just think, oh two girls, look good look good look good, and they think that's what they're paid to do. So we were unhappy with those things, but it's a drop in the ocean really.

I think Miki is more into the glamour of being in a band. She's definitely happier doing photo sessions than I am. I'm uncomfortable with it, I've had rows with make-up artists over wearing false eyelashes!

Miki's more confident in some ways and she's not in others. She's more gregarious and more able to get what she wants and I'm a bit scared to say things that might come out wrong. When we were younger I was her fat friend. Everyone fancied her and they didn't fancy me, and everyone recognised her because of her bright red hair, and I think when we got older I made a bit of a break from it. I made a new set of friends when she went to college. She was never, ever horrible to me at all but it happens. I overshadowed someone myself when I was younger. I made a conscious decision to break away from it. When we were at school she was brainier and prettier and I think with the band I took a lot of it more on board. I had ambition and I dealt with the administration and the songs more. But now it's not like that, although I still keep in control of my songs.

When you're in a band with people all these weird things go down although I think we get on really well which is unusual. There's no egos really.

I do like the idea of having men on stage with me, although I don't think I could be in a band with a male vocalist. I do like male vocalists, but I just prefer the sounds that women make. There are a lot of bands with terrible male vocalists but men can get away with singing badly more than women can. If a woman's got a shit voice it's awful. Not that women should sound pretty. I used to like Pauline Murray and she was really shouty, and Poly Styrene was good. Women can sound a lot more individual.

People who've never seen us say we try to sound like angel choirs, but if you listen to our first record, *Gala*, it's really raw. I just write music that I like and I think it's funny that people expect you to be a certain way because of your music. I get letters saying how much these people love me, but it's not so much, 'I want to shag you', it's much more like, 'Oh, you're some mysterious goddess' or something. I remember when we first started this bloke asked me if he could touch me! It's much more to do with idealisation than actual sex.

Some people have asked us whether we actually play on our records. Someone once said they heard that Robin Guthrie played on the second LP, *Spooky*. Well, yeah, so he put down a little keyboard part on something. So what? And once during the 1992 Lollapalooza tour of America, our guitar tech was tuning a guitar and someone thought he was playing my part at the side of the stage! I mean, if we were going to do that, he wouldn't be visible. Some people just want to believe those things, but we play everything.

Popular culture has quite a big influence on people. I mean, if I did what I was brought up to do, I'd be married with two kids and living in Sutton or something. If you look at rock music in general, I'm sure women who are involved influence people but not as much as they should. Sometimes you see yourself in your little world and you don't realise what's happening in other parts of the country, in other people's lives. There are still people who read *The Sun*!

When I was younger I thought things were going to change and the Tories were going to die, but they haven't. You get on the tube and there's 18-year-old boys looking at page 3 and it's really depressing. And you can go abroad and see where feminism hasn't done a thing. In some places women are pieces of shit. It's all very well reading Germaine Greer, but there is so much more shit. We're at a very early stage if you think back two hundred or even twenty years ago. It's a learning process.

I hope that some of our female fans would be inspired to think they could play in a band too, but over 50 per cent of the audiences are male. I think most audiences are, aren't they? I think it's changing though. We've had a few fanatical female fans. There were two in America who used to write us long letters asking us which one looked more like Miki and which one looked more like me!

I'm assuming that women do want to hear about female experiences. It's difficult to know what people think about or get from the songs. The trouble with a lot of our songs is you can't hear the words anyway! Our lyrics are important but they're the last things that are written. The music is more important definitely.

There is a weirdness towards women in music. I just think some people can't handle women expressing themselves. Women as much as men, because they're not used to it. I don't know what would have to be done for that not to happen anymore. Sometimes I think we shouldn't talk about women in rock, we should be out there doing it.

Miki Berenyi

I was brought up in a way that I think was completely unorthodox, and if I saw someone bringing their kids up like it now, I'd tell them they were wrong.

My parents were pretty irresponsible and pretty neglectful, but then they were also pretty young. My dad's a journalist, and he's still running round Hungary shagging young Russian girls. He's a great bloke but he's just totally irresponsible. And my mum has got a location business in Los Angeles and a fashion photographer's agency so she's always busy and she's a real socialite, but again she's not really the holy type. I used to admire them as people but as parents I thought they were fucking awful. It was all right once I could leave home, and I could look after myself, but when you're a kid you feel a bit helpless.

My mum had upper-class pretensions because she married this director, who worked on *The Professionals* and *Black Beauty* and *Space 1999* and things. He was a real Elephant and Castle wide boy but he wanted to escape his past. He was such a snob, always covered in really tasteless gold chains and signet rings!

When I was 11, my stepdad took my mum to America and she's always felt bad about going but I think well, yeah, she still went. My dad wouldn't let her take me anyway, and I didn't actually really want

37

to go. Can you imagine if I'd been brought up in Los Angeles? At the time I thought I could cope without her, but when I grew up I realised there were times when I really needed a mother, like starting my periods and just adolescence. I had to muddle through on my own, I didn't have a woman to turn to. Afterwards I really resented her for it, but then I thought, well, what was she supposed to do—give up her whole life just to stay in England and look after me? It was an unsolvable situation really. She'd have been miserable if she'd stayed which wouldn't have been any good for me anyway.

So I lived with my dad, but he'd bugger off for absolutely months and I'd be left with my lunatic Hungarian grandmother who was just crazy. She was a Nazi! I've just found out that her brother really was a Nazi in South America too. I remember I used to watch *Colditz* with her and she'd say, 'Lies, lies!' And she thought Emma was Jewish and she'd be saying 'Get that Jew out!' in Hungarian whenever Emma came round! So I got left with her and basically by the age of 11 I had to look after myself, doing all the shopping and cooking, and I was lonely because when you're that young, you can't really share that kind of thing with friends because they'd think you were a bit weird.

I suppose I was constantly lying about home to fit in. I remember saying my parents were divorced at one school I went to, and they all pitied me because it wasn't that common then, so I thought, well I won't say that again! You try and make up this family life so that everyone likes you and thinks you're normal. It's a bit weird with children. People go on about how great it was to be a child, but when you think about the things that embarrassed you then, and the way you took things on yourself, it wasn't always that great.

It's a bit of a crappy subject now because everyone goes on about it so much, but I used to suffer an element of child abuse, because my

parents were never there. I think if I had a kid I'd know that something had happened to them, just from the way they were behaving. But my parents weren't really around so they didn't notice, and I had this fucking mad grandmother who did some weird things to me, but I couldn't talk about it with my dad.

When I was 8 I went through a phase when I couldn't speak to people. I'd go into shops with the exact change because I just couldn't bear to have to hear my own voice, and I used to walk everywhere because I couldn't bear to get on a bus and have to say 'Half please'.

What annoys me about a lot of what's written about child abuse is it's always about some girl being put upon by these oily disgusting men. In my experience it wasn't like that at all. By the time I'd got to 11, I'd blocked most of it out, and once one of the blokes turned up when I was living with my dad and there was this flood of recognition and I just slammed the door in his face. But it wasn't like I was horrified that he had done something to me, I was embarrassed that I had behaved like that once, like I was some kind of slag. I felt guilty.

You know what little girls are like—'Ooh look at my knickers!'—and I thought it must have been my fault and that I must have encouraged him, and I did this and I did that, so I wouldn't tell anyone, because it was like me being dirty, rather than someone doing it to me. You are made to feel that it's your fault.

I think one of the effects of child abuse is that, depending on the circumstances, obviously, it often makes children really precocious, especially if the abuser is someone the family knows. In a way, child abuse is paying a child more attention than it should be paid and because kids don't know about sex, they think, ooh, this man wants to play with me. And it makes children precocious in the same way that adult attention full stop does. It makes them constantly attention seeking. I've noticed that women who've been abused can grow up to

be very promiscuous because they're constantly seeking that same attention, and they'll sleep with anyone to get it. They become sex victims rather than aggressors.

I think all the talk surrounding it has changed the awareness of child abuse, although it's dangerous to hold onto it as though it makes you an exceptional person. To say that I'm in a band and I'm successful because I was abused as a child would obviously be ridiculous, although I think it's better for people to see how common it is and that actually so many people suffer from it because the worst part of it is that when you're a child, it makes you feel abnormal. It makes you think that no one else at school is going through it so you feel like some kind of freak. And then, even worse, some children start to feel proud of it because that's their way of dealing with it, but they don't really know what they're getting themselves into.

People have different ways of dealing with it and I do think it's very common. Something like one in four children is being abused sexually and I think those people use their experiences in different ways. They can use it once they're a singer or a painter, they can put images of it and memories of it into what they do, but I don't think it should be used as some sort of inspiration exactly.

Treating children as partners even if there isn't any physical stuff going on is pretty strange too. My dad used to do that to me. I mean, he'd take me to nightclubs and I'd pick up his girlfriends for him. He'd tell me to go and speak to them and then he'd come over and get me. And I used to really hate all of them because I was so possessive of him. He laughs about it now, and says, 'Oh I remember when so and so came round and you said, "You fucking Austrian whore" or something, and I get so embarrassed. Those poor women! But then I think, well it's his fucking fault, he was always going on about his little girl.

I ended up being really introvert until I was 13 and I broke down. I'd always had to think about my identity because I was always being ferried around between different schools, and with the abuse and having to fend for myself I couldn't cope anymore. My headmistress said, 'Look you're obviously having problems, so do you want to live in the school for a bit?' Until I moved into the school hostel, I had a camp bed in the music room!

I was all right then, because I met Emma and I got into music. We had these friends and together we were this bunch of misfits who felt we were so unattractive that we could never even think about boys so we just rejected them from the start. So while everyone else was mooning over Constantine from Westminster College or someone, we were mooning over David Sylvian!

None of us had brothers or sisters so we had to start at the pop end and work our way down to the more independent stuff. When you first get into a band it's because you fancy the lead singer apart from Blondie and the Banshees, because I was totally into Debbie Harry and I was totally into Siouxsie Sioux.

We started going to smaller and smaller gigs, and by the time we got to these gigs we didn't feel threatened by the fact that it was all blokes in the bands, although I think if there hadn't been any women at all I'd have noticed. I think maybe if you're older, twenty-something, you're more conscious of your limitations as a woman and then it bothers you that there aren't more female role models, but not when you're 16.

People are going on now about all these women in bands, but there always have been, even if they're little pathetic bands that you never hear of again. There were loads of goth bands like Skeletal Family or whoever, and All About Eve even, so there were loads of bands with girls in. And then there were people like the Shop

Assistants, but at that age you don't think, oh it's great to see a woman on stage, I can really relate to that; you think, oh I can do that.

Emma joined a band before I did. She was in the Rover Girls with Chris and Stuart who are now in Silverfish. I used to go and see all these little garage bands and The Bugs were one of them. I'd met them a few times and they told me their bass player was leaving for San Francisco and I was pissed out of my mind at this pub one night and I was going, 'Oh I'll play bass for you!' One of them was saying, 'Really?' and I thought no way, he's winding me up. The next day I'd forgotten all about it and he rang me up and asked me to a rehearsal. I had a week to learn to play bass—I'd never played in my life! I was going out with this bloke who played guitar, and he worked out all the songs for me, so I could memorise them. I went to this rehearsal and I thought, God this is a piece of piss! We went on tour and we were rubbish but it was quite good fun.

Me and Emma had always had this idea of being in a band together though, and we used to fuck around at her house. We were called Baby Machine to begin with, but we never did anything under that name, we just pissed around in Emma's kitchen. I think Emma was probably the more serious, I think she really wanted it to work and if it hadn't been for her we'd have ended up like The Frank and Walters, but not even that good. We'd be like some sort of joke band. I was quite happy to bang out any old rubbish and just enjoy myself, whereas Emma was more picky about the songs, so it started to shape up a bit. Then I met Chris at college and I asked him if he wanted to play drums with us and he said OK, so then we had to write some songs! Meriel, who's in the Pale Saints now, was at college too, so she was singing.

Colleges are good for gigging actually. There's a bunch of girls who come to our gigs, they're about 15 or 16 and they say they don't want to bother with 'A' levels because they just want to get into music. And I say, 'Well, you know the best fucking thing you can do is to go to college because you've got so much free time! I did eight hours a week at college and never bothered with all the homework. We used to go touring in the middle of term, it was brilliant! We toured with the House of Love during our finals!

I think I always took it seriously enough to play and want to tour but I'm still not willing to crawl up my own ass about how important our music is for the continuation of the cosmos. I just think, well, look, it's a laugh. Yes, there is a serious element to it and we work to make music and it excites us and it moves us, but I'm not going to sit here and say 'Oh, music is my life!' It is a laugh to me in the sense that I enjoy doing it and I don't have any solid ambitions to play Wembley Stadium.

When Meriel left we had to advertise to get someone in and we got all these phone calls from utterly unsuitable maniacs. Half of them were mad and the other half were professionals wanting to know how much money they were going to make from it. In the end either we were going to have to sing, or we were going to have to split up. Emma said 'No way', and the reason I had to sing in the end was because I'd been doing some backing vocals. When I say backing vocals I mean a noise which was in the same key as the one everyone was playing. I couldn't even play guitar properly, let alone sing and play guitar but by then we'd already started playing gigs, so I had to learn on stage. It wasn't like I could spend a couple of years becoming a singer and guitarist!

Boys are always encouraged to play guitars and they can hide behind their instruments. You can't be a singer without a band, but you can practise guitar on your own to records, feel like you're getting somewhere and then join a band by the time you're 17.

Girls don't have the patience to spend six years learning someone else's music. Me and Emma still can't jam because we only know how to play our own songs. Jamming's more of a boy's thing. The actual proficiency at playing an instrument is very much tied up in what people choose to play and girls don't show off as much basically. They're not so much like trick cyclists. I think that women play more imaginatively because they learn to play while they're writing songs, instead of waiting to be technically good first.

We had press attention almost straight away and I think it was partly because we had two girls in the band. That in itself irritated me because then people started saying that the only reason we got press was because there were two girls in the band and I'd say, well, initially yes, but I'm not going to let someone take away my fucking glory by saying that's the only reason. I find it a bit insulting. It was also partly because we lived in London so all our gigs were central and it was partly because we knew so many people, including journalists, who we'd known from when they'd written for fanzines—we'd done a fanzine too, called *Alphabet Soup*. By the time we'd started the band they were all writing for the inky press, so we were getting reviews way too early. We were shit because we hadn't spent much time rehearsing.

Right at the start no one wanted to talk to Chris and Steve, and I suppose we wanted to suppress the fact that we were girls as much as possible, not because we were ashamed of being women, but because we didn't want to be separated off for being women. But I suppose we over-compensated for it. If you actually look at male bands, everyone wants to talk to the songwriters, they're not interested in the drummer!

I don't think in the end we were actually treated that differently because we were women, although one male journalist slagged us off by saying he'd never seen two women so controlled by men—male producers and managers and record label bosses—in his life. I thought that was a sexist statement in itself because if you look at any young band, whether they're men or women, they usually have male managers and so on.

Now we sometimes say no to things our label or our manager ask us to do, but only because we're older and wiser. In the beginning we had to work our asses off and do everything. It's got nothing to do with being little girls and being told which dresses to wear. People don't say that Primal Scream are controlled by Andy Weatherall, because they're a bunch of lads, so it's all right. But if we had an Andy Weatherall type transform all our records into dance music we'd have been called little girl puppets.

You don't really encounter that much sexism if you behave in a certain way. Not that people ask for it, but I find it a bit ironic when women complain about the sort of treatment they get from industry people or whoever, when they're willing to wear tiny clothes and they're trying to make out that they're some kind of sexy woman. I think that the idea of someone doing a *Playboy* centre spread and saying 'Well, I did it because I'm showing that women can have control of their bodies and they should enjoy their bodies' is bollocks! How many women read *Playboy* anyway? I think it's a very easy thing to be beautiful, and want everyone to fancy you, I think it's so easy to do that and too many women try and justify it, but I think it's rubbish.

Let's face it, me and Emma are fairly ordinary-looking girls, but when we did the video for 'Nothing Natural' we looked fantastic, and I hated it, I thought it was so boring. There was no character or expression in those faces, it was just me and Emma looking pretty.

That doesn't subvert anything, any subversion goes on in your head, with your own justification. Even Madonna's book, *Sex* was only relevant because it was her and she's such a unique case. If anyone else did that it would just be loads of naked pictures of someone.

When I saw *Sex* I also thought it was for men. I don't like really beautiful images of women when they're lies, which they generally are. She probably went on a diet beforehand so she'd look thin in the photographs, and those kinds of images are always airbrushed and lit in a certain way and they actually make women feel more insecure about themselves. Even when they're having sex, some women don't actually enjoy the sex, because they're worried about how they look. I've heard blokes when they're being a bit rowdy, talking about people they'd slept with, saying things like 'God she kept putting her arms over her head, trying to make her tits look really nice, and it was really annoying 'cos I wanted her to hold onto me.' I think that's quite common, and those images alienate women, rather than make them feel that they want to do that. I think it's really difficult to rethink your aesthetic responses in that way.

So many women feel that they want to be beautiful and their dream is to be on some kind of magazine cover, and everyone will think she's gorgeous and that men'll fancy her and women will be jealous. There's a great temptation to be on the front cover of the *Melody Maker* or the *NME* looking like a complete stunner and wear revealing clothes on stage, but I don't think it's powerful if you want to be a musician, because it reduces you to being judged by how you look and not by how you play. And women get enough of that as it is.

A lot of blokes go on about women in bands being really ugly. I remember there was a feature on women in rock in some music paper and there was a big picture of Polly Harvey surrounded by quotes from people about her. The main quote was, 'I think she's really ugly, I bet she's never been shagged.' I thought how dare someone say that. They've obviously got a problem. And why did the paper print it in such massive letters? It was so crap and so cruel. If you constantly batter at someone you do break them down, it's hurtful.

Women who get their kits off aren't thinking about other women at all. I remember when Madonna was still wearing her cut-off top and her crucifixes and Suzanne Vega said, 'Well, it's all right for Madonna, but all these little girls who copy her are just going to look like a bunch of sluts.' It's the same with page 3 girls saying they're the ones with all the power and the money, but what about the rest of us who have to stand on the tube while some bloke is gawping at the paper and then looking at us and saying, 'All right, love'? I think it affects all women.

I don't like pornography, it actually makes me feel uncomfortable. They won't allow child pornography on moral grounds but they allow 16-year-old girls in those magazines. Because it generally concerns women, what can you do? It makes you identify with those women, lying there, feeling vulnerable, and having loads of blokes taking the piss out of you. I don't like it at all. I won't have it on the bus at all on tour.

I think it's difficult to try and change peoples' opinions about women in general by just being a successful woman in the music business. Supposedly Madonna bends over backwards to subvert every sexual stereotype that there is, but no one ever applies that to the general public, they just think, oh that's Madonna. I think you'd probably find that if you go back in history you'll always find women who've made an impact, like Siouxsie Sioux and Patti Smith, and whether in films or art or music or writing there have always been people like that, and that's not what changes things. What really changes things are women getting equal pay, economic movements of women having to work, and getting more successful jobs. Individual women making an impact are still seen as different from the rest. So if I become tremendously successful, and 50 people go out and dye their hair red, no one's going to think they must be really independent as well, they're going to think, oh look at that silly cow with the red hair!

I think a lot of people think that feminism was born in the 1970s and that from then on it's been rising on an upward scale. Well, that's bollocks! If you look back over history, the Victorian era was far worse than the previous era, and it's been up and down, up and down all the way through. It's not a rising scale. Never mind that everyone was going to Riot Grrl meetings last year, and everyone was into grunge fashion and not wearing make up, you can guarantee that this year we'll be back to girls wearing hotpants with the crack of their ass showing and Kylie Minogue throwing herself around like a 12-year-old nymphette! It's just fashion. When I was younger there were The Au Pairs and Delta 5 and all these bands that sang quite ardently about women's issues, and I used to love The Au Pairs, because they were a bit over the top. A lot of their lyrics were totally man-hating. And then the Shop Assistants came along and the scene was full of little girls with Pastels badges on. It works in waves, it hasn't been a steady climbing scale at all.

When Shakespears Sister were at number one with 'Stay' there was an article in *The Guardian* which really pissed me off. The journalist, who was female by the way, was citing Shakespears Sister as the pinnacle for all of women in rock throughout history, and that Patti Smith was just a bit kooky and Debbie Harry was just a puppet and Siouxsie was just a dressed-up marionette. I thought, how the hell can you say that? What an insult! I thought, there's no way that a man would write about Suede being the pinnacle of male achievement and that Nick Cave was just some sort of weirdo and Bryan Ferry was just a perfumed ponce!

Everyone I know has got a very different idea of what feminism is. To me this whole thing about women in bands inspiring other women in bands, Courtney Love being slagged off because she called someone fat and me and Emma not being real feminists because we've got two blokes in the band and a male manager, just detracts from the real issue. My problem with the whole gender issue is that I don't think women like each other very much. I think, well, fuck men, they're obviously not going to be very sympathetic towards women because they're not women but what I think is tragic is that women will do anything to put each other down. If a bloke sits there and says 'I think Madonna's a right dog,' a lot of women will say 'Oh yes, she's got a bit of cellulite actually.' I mean for God's sake! It's all tied up with by-products of patriarchal culture but I can't believe that women are so stupid that they fall for that kind of thing.

I could understand it if women couldn't work or if they were invalid in some sense and that they did have to fight over men so they could get a life by getting married. But they don't have to anymore. If you sit back and think, why am I in competition with these women in here, what do I want to achieve, it becomes pointless. If you think, well, why do I want every man in this room to fancy me, you realise that you can't go out with them all at the same time and you probably don't fancy them anyway. That's what annoys me about girls who get all bitchy and say things like, 'Well she's a bit fat isn't she?' I mean, who cares? And that's why I don't like women who encourage girls to want to be the prettiest. I think if they encouraged them to be something else, to stick together a bit more, it'd be so much more worthwhile.

In that sense I think me and Emma being in a band together offers a good image, because it shows that girls can play together without worrying about which one of them looks better in the fucking photographs! They just make music and they're friends. People even try and get me and Emma to separate! They write letters saying which one of us they like best and which one they think is the prettier! As if we're going to be flattered or start hating each other!

I don't think we started the band because we wanted to reveal ourselves as women, we did it because we wanted to be in a band. Lyrically, our first songs were these very naïve feminist anthems, with very basic politics and sloganeering. When you're young you think you're the first person to have discovered those things and you get a bit arrogant about it. We soon realised that most of those things had been said much better by other people though!

I think now we write about things that only women really know about. All the songs are expressions of being women, because they're our personal viewpoints, and we don't write flip lyrics like 'Baby, I love you so'. Our words do have a relevant emotional content or they are specifically about things which have happened. I think it's fairly hard for blokes to relate to those lyrics, although they tell us that they do. We don't do it consciously, it's just us.

I think we used to be embarrassed about our lyrics really. We do work at them and I think the frustration people have had with not being able to hear them has been justified. This woman, Betty Page, reviewed our album *Spooky* for the *NME* and she said it was a shame we didn't print our lyrics when there are so few women writing interesting words anyway. I thought she had a point. Why should we be embarrassed to print them if we can be bothered to sing them? We will print them in future, because it's not as if we write anything inane or without a purpose.

People think that women don't write songs as well as men and that's why it's been The Beatles and The Rolling Stones and Elvis all these years and it's obviously ridiculous. It's just what's been popularised, but when you're young, you don't really question it. You just accept the male point of view even when it means nothing to you personally. It's the kind of marginalisation which goes on in life for women all the time.

In music, if you're female you're always marginalised politically. There was a time not long ago when if you weren't angry in a very obvious way, screaming your head off like Courtney Love or Kat Bjelland, then you weren't valid, you weren't a whole woman. This journalist totally stitched us up in the *NME* for not being 'political' enough. He started off by asking us about Baby Machine and our earliest lyrics, and I told him that they'd been really bad feminist things written from a completely naïve viewpoint. Their only appeal was that we were young and unable to express ourselves better, which is really what Riot Grrl was about. He said that they sounded brilliant, much better than what we were doing now, and of course he hadn't heard any of them at all!

I don't think you have to sing about party politics to be political. If a song is moving it has much more effect. Marianne Faithfull did this song called 'Why D'Ya Do It?' and it's so nasty and bitter, it's scary and that's more political. When you get a really honest song that hits the nerve, it's so much more effective than sloganeering. I think it takes more guts for a woman to write a song where she admits that she finds other women a threat than it is for her to sham it and say 'Oh I love all other women' because nobody loves everybody, it's a lie.

A lot of people like their politics expressed in very black and white terms though. You know, like in order to be a real, political woman you have to not wear make up. It's fucking rubbish. Politics are about individual people, not a herd mentality. Half our songs are about what pisses us off, and a lot of that is the kind of treatment we might have as women, the kind of treatment I might have being half-Japanese and half-Hungarian, or something to do with being from a certain social class, but I wouldn't write a song declaring that I hate everyone who votes Tory because I don't and that would be a ridiculous thing to say. And I'm not going to write a song saying all men are wankers because I don't think they are.

People expect your music to reflect your personality in the most obvious ways too. Because we make this airy fairy music, me and Emma are expected to be these nice little girls, like angels on a Christmas tree! So if I'm pissed out of my head in a pub and acting like an idiot, it crops up in the press as if I'm a fucking asshole. People think I'm this monster maniac, and they're really fascinated by the discrepancy between our music and the type of people we are. I'm no different to half the people who get pissed and go to gigs. And I'm not a real tomboy because I watch football, although the press have made me out to be one. I know as much about it as any other couch potato who can't be bothered to switch the telly over! Still, it's not as bad as the treatment other women get. Tanya Donelly is made out to be this sweet little thing, and she is sweet and she is little, but there's so much more to her than than. She writes fucking brilliant songs for a start!

We've always been totally against the idea of image, we didn't cultivate one because all the bands we'd liked had images but not cultivated ones. But you always have an image. I used to get people coming up to me and asking me why I told stupid jokes on stage because it ruined the image they had of me. They'd say things like 'You play this beautiful song and at the end of it you say "Well that was a load of bollocks wasn't it?" I suppose people think it's a bit common, but I could never take myself that seriously. I suppose it's all a matter of confidence though. Even people in quite raucous bands say they couldn't do what I do in between songs, but really I'm hiding just as much as someone who cultivates a huge, mysterious image. It's quite basic—people want to be liked, whether by wearing sexy clothes, telling jokes, or being enigmatic. It all amounts to the same thing.

When I was growing up I thought I was pig ugly and Emma thought she was, too, and it's quite common for people to turn themselves into the class clown in order to be liked. I could never think of myself as standing on stage and being so beautiful that it would be enough for people just to look at me. So I justify my presence by entertaining people a bit. The downside of being matey on stage is that people want you to speak to them. I used to get really angry about it when it got abusive, but I think in a way I dug my own grave because now people do it just to get a response.

I saw Tanya Donelly handle some verbal abuse really well once. Someone said something like, 'Ooh, get your clothes off!' and she just turned round and said, 'Well that's brilliant isn't it? You're just this anonymous person in the crowd. Why don't you get up here and say that? You're such a gutless little creep, hiding down there in the darkness!'

There are a lot of itchy little boys who burst into tears the second you pay any attention to them, but they obviously go back to school and tell all their friends they've shagged you! I've had plenty of that. And you get a lot of creepy people too, especially in America.

In America I was pretty shocked by the groupies. They're very business-like and they just stand by the gates and get their tits out for the security guys so they can get backstage. They drop their pants and say things like, 'Well, do you wanna do it now?' It's revolting!

There's a very broad spectrum of groupies, and the popular conception is that all blokes love them, but plenty of men hate groupies. They don't like being pawed by anonymous women and they get bored with their conversation in exactly the same way as women do when these idiotic boys come backstage. There are a lot of female groupies involved who don't actually want to fuck anyone either. For them it's not about bed, it's about walking around the shopping centre, in a kind of 'Look who I'm with!' way. Half of them would run away if sex ever came up!

Some blokes in bands like the idea of some little innocent who they can corrupt, but a lot don't like sexual aggression. It's down to their attitudes really. I don't think many women are that interested in the prospect of a quivering 17-year-old boy though, because if they extend that to the bedroom, they know it'll only last for a second, and the boy's going to be useless because he's scared!

The fans I like are the ones you can have a conversation with. Real fandom can be a bit hard to handle because I don't seek out adulation from individual people. Some people love that kind of power but it just irritates me.

I sometimes get girls coming up to me at gigs and it's really heartening because I don't alienate them like some of these really beautiful women do. I think Toni Halliday's really good because she's got all these blokes thinking she's sexy but at the same time she doesn't make other women feel ugly in comparison.

I used to think Debbie Harry was fantastic. She was beautiful and she used to wear dodgy clothes but I never felt threatened by her beauty because I never felt that I had to look like her to be in a band. I resent people slagging women off if they're in a band and they happen to be beautiful even though they're talented. Although a lot of the time pop is about perfect homogenous images and girls get into pop music when they're young, so their role models are the ones who get on the television like Kylie Minogue and all these other women who don't write their own music. And if they do it's just a backbeat with a bunch of inane words over the top and anyone can do that. For young girls music is more to do with sex symbols and pop personalities than artistic effort.

I remember once I was interviewed for a piece on women in rock by the *NME*, and I got loads of flak for slagging off Kylie Minogue. The week after the interview was printed, the letters page had been edited completely against my favour, by a woman. All the letters were saying I was just jealous of Kylie because she was prettier than me, and what a shame it is that women knock each other. Well, the thing is that I think Kylie looks great, and I haven't got a problem with her in that department, but I do have a problem with *NME* journalists and bands like Primal Scream and the Manic Street Preachers saying that women in rock should all be like Kylie. They were so obviously threatened. If there weren't so many strong women making music they wouldn't have bothered mentioning her at all. They obviously thought there were all these women like Courtney Love and Polly Harvey and Kat Bjelland around, and that women were getting a bit too serious, so they chose to elevate a complete idiot to the top of the scale. They did the same thing with Wendy James and where is she now? And they were saying how power crazy Madonna was. I thought, well how can they say that when everything Kylie does is a complete rip off of Madonna!

I think women are ghettoised in a way if they go on about women's issues, but you have to because it affects all women. You don't have a terrible time being a woman in a band, but there is a difference that people have to be aware of, just as in everyday life there's a difference. Women are treated differently. It's not about having a hard time or getting depressed, it's purely about the difference. The thing that pisses me off is when all women in all bands are expected to be one thing. We are never allowed to co-exist, and that would never happen with men.

Credentials

Band:	Lush
Signed to:	4AD in Britain, Reprise in America
Managed by:	Howard Gough
Past bands:	Emma Anderson—The Rover Girls
	Miki Berenyi—The Bugs
Select discography:	*Scar* EP (1989)
	Mad Love EP (1990)
	Sweetness And Light EP (1990)
	Spooky LP (1992)
	Split LP (1994)

Kat Bjelland Gray

'*P*eople really aren't used to women expressing the
kinds of things we do. Just because I'm screaming
doesn't mean I'm screaming out of anger, I could
be screaming out of passion or frustration.'

Kat Bjelland Gray

Introduction

With her baby blonde curls, her second-hand dresses and her bright red screams, Kat Bjelland Gray has sworn new life into female passion. Her earsplitting shrieks and strangled guitar playing have shattered existing pain barriers, forcing female expression into startling shape. She exposes woman's body as a battleground with lyrics of grave intensity, ripping up the clean facades which disfigure contradiction and conflict, and paints female experience in savage shades beneath an unforgiving spotlight. Stamping her feet on stage, bashing the edge of her guitar against her bruised hips, whirling her head like a demon, Bjelland Gray uncovers nerve endings in all their tangled glory. Like a kick in the teeth, she reminds people of an uncultured female spirit and unsurprisingly has often been jammed up inside descriptive cages which try very hard to shrink her.

Estranged from her biological parents at the age of three, Bjelland Gray grew up in Oregon with her stepfather and his abusive wife. She was often locked up in her room where, left to her own imaginings, she developed a private world which formed the basis of the inner life she now draws on for songwriting.

On moving to Portland, Bjelland Gray met Courtney Love, who now plays with Hole and is the widow of Nirvana's Kurt Cobain.

The two bonded immediately and moved to San Francisco to form Sugar Baby Doll with Jennifer Finch, currently the bass player with Los Angeles band L7.

Bjelland Gray felt completely alienated in California, and took off for Minneapolis where she met Lori Barbero and Michelle Leon and formed Babes in Toyland, initially with Love on vocals. When Bjelland Gray kicked her friend out of the band, a rift widened between the two for several years, sustained by professional rivalry and their strong feelings for each other, which Love once described as 'romantic'.

Sticking close to the principle of punk, Babes In Toyland were a raw, instinctive trio who grew up in public and yelled their way out of the underground scene, across America and all the way to Europe. An independent record deal in 1989 enabled them to commit themselves to vinyl and in 1992 they linked up with a major company in the States, by which time Leon had been replaced by local musician Maureen Herman.

Now married to Stuart Gray, a musician from Seattle, Bjelland Gray has completed with her husband an album called *Crunt*, and is hoping to work again with Courtney Love at some point.

Babes In Toyland's brave, stark tunnellings into the stickier end of female emotions have earned them outrageous reactions from all quarters of the music press. Bjelland Gray's openly vicious lyrics which swing moods by the tail and twist nasty wishes out of thin air, have fundamentally upset rock's careful expeditions into humanity's dark side by blazing a female trail of unashamed bitchiness. Girls are not supposed to be this nasty, and when they are, as Bjelland's experience has proved, they are 'horror shows', tantrum-toting, red-faced brats, caterwauling banshees or ball-breaking psychos.

The myths which have sprung up around female anger are astonishing. From the stony glare of Medusa to Shakespeare's belief that 'Hell hath no fury ...' right up to modern movies like *Fatal Attraction*, female anger has been feared and distorted into something purely evil. Bjelland Gray's expressions are deemed even more sinister because of her sugary-sweet looks, but if anything, this serves to undermine the 'niceness' of girls who often bear no resemblance to the pretty picture afforded by their frills and flounces.

In blowing up the boundaries of acceptable female emotion, Bjelland Gray reminds people that if women are to be understood and appreciated as human beings, they must be given the rights to express everything they feel, whether good or really, really bad. Angry women are not hysterical bitches, neurotics or necessarily premenstrual. They're angry, and there's nothing horrific about that.

Kat Bjelland Gray

In Her Own Words

When I was about three years old, my mom gave me to my stepdad, because I got sick, and she was a really poor hippy in San Francisco and couldn't take care of me. At the time I thought he was my real dad, 'cos I had got used to them being married. I didn't find out about my real dad until I was 18, which was weird. I was like 'Huh? I have a different dad?! I'm not Norwegian?!' You know how you grow up thinking you're from a certain family? So I'm English and German—but it doesn't really matter. I didn't actually meet my dad till I was 23, and he came to see my band at the Satyricon club in Portland.

I kind of kept in touch with my mother and I have all these half brothers and sisters all over the place. I went up to New York before she died, and that was a really weird time. Our record *To Mother* has her picture on the cover from when she was a little girl. It was like a tribute to her. She was really cool, I wish I had got to know her a lot better, but she got cancer.

My stepdad married this other woman Judy, my stepmom, and I grew up in a small town in Oregon with them. The only weird thing that really happened to me a lot was that I used to get grounded constantly when I was little. I was locked into my room all the time. I'm pretty sure that being grounded and locked up has a lot to do with the way my imagination developed. You have to think up ways to entertain yourself, make up a place that's better. Now I get really claustrophobic. The other day I got stuck in an elevator and I was in there for about 15 minutes, hanging off the walls. I didn't feel really bad until I got out and I was shaking. It's the worst, it is so scary, it makes you mental.

Also when I was young, I thought I was evil and that no one liked me. If you have an abusive mother you think that it's because parents know best. I don't talk about it in interviews, but I was beaten up a lot by my stepmom. My stepdad was oblivious to it, but I used to hide behind doors until he came home. He was working all day so he couldn't stop anything anyway, and when I told him about it he thought I'd been exaggerating, but in a way I think he knew because he was always nicer to me than to his own daughters.

I didn't really have any schoolfriends because my best friend was a year younger than me and at school that makes a big difference. There was this little clique of girls that I always wanted to be friends with but they would never come to my house 'cos my mom was too mean.

When I was in eighth grade I got picked to be a cheerleader. Until I was 13 I'd always felt ugly, so maybe it built my confidence up. I always wanted to look like my best friend Jackie. She's Philippino and Indonesian, and she was really beautiful, she still is.

So things got better in high school, but of course as soon as everyone started liking me I started rejecting everybody. It was like 'I always wanted to be popular and now I don't!' It was a total switch.

In tenth grade, when I was 15, I started going out with a musician who was eight years older than me and he was the best. When I was about 19 I used to mess around on his guitar, and he said I should play 'cos I was a natural. I said I could never play guitar! I always wanted to but I was chicken. I had asked for a guitar in second grade, but it was a classical so the neck was too big and I couldn't play it.

During my last year at school, I missed five weeks out of a nine-week period, because I was hanging out with my boyfriend and all these older people, and getting more into music but I passed because I was good at sports. I was always in the local paper 'cos I did track and played basketball, but then, as my parents said, I went bad. I dyed my hair black and cut it all weird and sat down at dinner and acted like nothing was going on.

I started to play in my Uncle David's surf band, The Neurotics, when I was about 19. He's my real mom's brother and he was kind of like a hippy so my stepparents thought he was crazy. We used to practise in his living room, and I had to play rhythm guitar, because I couldn't play too well at all. I'd been messing around with guitar during the one term I spent at college, but I'd driven my room mate nuts, so I quit classes and stayed at home practising, which is when I got serious about it.

After The Neurotics I got this band together with my best friends, so it was an all-girl band. We were called The Venarays. The name came from the word 'venary' which means actively hunting out sex! We began as a way of having fun with each other. Men always wait until they're perfect before they go out into the world, but women tend to just go out anyway, 'cos they know they're perfect!

I'd always been into music, but I was from such a small town and there was no good radio, so the only way you could find out about anything was through the local drug store, or the record store. I discovered The Plasmatics and the B52s, 'cos of their album covers. I didn't know who they were but I liked the way they looked. I liked Wendy O'Williams and Chrissie Hynde, and then I saw Girlschool and I thought shit! I didn't know that girls could do that! I saw them with Mötörhead and Ozzy Osbourne I think. I was really into metal, I was a total smalltown metalhead person on a riot! And then I moved to Portland with The Venarays and started going to clubs and getting into underground stuff.

It was in Portland that I met Courtney Love through the singer of a local band called The Miracle Workers. He introduced us at the Satyricon club and I got together with her the next day. She took me over to her house and we drank wine, took Valium, did some artwork and ran around the house. She tried to wash my face for me because I have this really bad habit of drinking and going to sleep with my make up on, so I learned how to take care of my skin from her which was a good thing!

When I met her she was really cool and energetic and vibrant, and we were really close from then on. It was like finding a soulmate, a sister-type person. That's why we've fallen out so badly in the past, but we're friends now. She got mad when I kicked her out of Babes In Toyland, but I kicked her out because I get mad too!

We started stripping together in Portland, and I worked at Mary's Club. It was the only job which allowed me to travel and work my own hours while making enough money to do exactly what I wanted to do.

It all seemed really burlesque to me, I wore diamond paste and rhinestones and G-strings, and I was really into it. I used to dance in five-inch heels and I never fell down which was weird 'cos I used to start drinking at noon. It probably turned me into kind of a lush actually. I was in good shape though. And you actually had to dance really well to a song there, you couldn't just strip. The men would tip you to dance in front of them which was horrible, I never got used to it. It didn't make me hate them at all, but it made me see a weird side of people.

In America, strip clubs are more for partying at, but there are sleazy places that I tried not to work in 'cos I couldn't take the brain damage. One time I freaked 'cos there was 14 dollars on the stage and I just ripped them all up and walked away. It makes you more aware of how you can wrap people round your finger and it's probably made me more aware of the body, which has probably influenced my lyrics, because the whole time I've been in a band I've been stripping. I started both at the same time. So I guess it's probably affected me a lot.

After a while me and Courtney caught this U haul, which was more like a hell haul, and went down to San Francisco to stay with her dad, Hank Harrison. He's a pretty interesting character. He's written a book on the Grateful Dead called *The Dead* and another one about the Goddamned Holy Grail! Anyway we met Jennifer Finch (who now plays bass with L7) there. I think Courtney knew her from Los Angeles.

I'd quit The Venarays by this time and me and Courtney were trying to get a band together. We needed a bass player, so when we found Jennifer we formed Sugar Baby Doll, Sugar Babylon, Sugar Bunny Farm or whatever it was called. We went through a few names, and we only played a couple of shows. It was the smallest thing I've ever done musically.

I guess I was floating around lost in those days, I'd never moved out of Oregon before and San Francisco was completely weird, I was getting really freaked out and agoraphobic and I didn't want to do anything. I didn't have any money and Courtney was helping me out with money from her trust fund, and we had this really big beautiful mansion on Fillmore Street which I found. I started getting really fucked up on speed then and I got so skinny it was disgusting. I thought I was going crazy.

Courtney went down to Los Angeles to try out for the *Sid and*

Nancy film, and ended up acting in Alex Cox's movie, *Straight To Hell*. That was when I left San Francisco and I did it without telling her 'cos I wanted to escape. I love her dearly but she can take over your life and I had to do something of my own.

I didn't know anybody in Minneapolis so I decided to move there. I liked the music of The Replacements and Soul Asylum, and I thought the mid West was kind of groovy. All the grubby boys came from there, all the flannel grunge, way before Seattle. The only person I knew there was a girlfriend I had known in college and I hadn't kept in touch with her, but it was kind of a reference point.

I would go to town and try to find out where all the cool people went. I used to go to this bar and sit there drinking, watching everybody. I would see Lori around, dancing and laughing and kicking up her heels. She was really animated and you could always hear her! She's really physical, she likes to hug people a lot. I seriously thought she had really good rhythm when I saw her dancing around, and that she could probably drum her ass off, it was like I could see potential.

Soon after I met Lori, we went for a picnic, and I found out she had a drumset, but she didn't know how to play. I thought, what the hell, all the people in my other bands couldn't 'play' either! I kind of look for that on purpose, it makes everything unique when people don't have previous training. Michelle Leon, Babes In Toyland's first bass player, didn't know how to play either.

We were shitty in the beginning and we didn't care. We had the right idea. It was super punk rock. I wasn't nervous when I started playing. I'd already been stripping! If I could take my clothes off, I could definitely play this guitar in front of people. It was just fun. It's more nerve wracking now actually because people expect us to be really good!

I do think women play differently to men. I think they do less guitar leads for one, which drive me up the wall. Women put less of that widdly show-off stuff into their songs—like 'This is how fast I can go!' Who said fast was good anyway? Why not just play a nice song without any of that stuff? I always pretend I can do that, but I'm just faking! I do this thing called a knifeslide where I bend my guitar and it makes this really cool noise. I learned that from my first boyfriend who had a Flying V. I have bruises all over my hips and stomach from hitting my guitar and bending it!

Sometimes my voice scares me when I'm playing live because I lose myself and I don't know what's going on. This guy was interviewing me after the 1993 Reading Festival and he said 'You seem really frightening—is that theatrical?' I felt like strangling him! I mean what did he want? What did he mean? I was so mad at him I didn't answer any more questions, I just stared at him. I've never had anyone ask me that before. Why would anyone want to be theatrical anyway? I wasn't really sure what he meant but I took it as an insult!

People really aren't used to women expressing the kind of things we do, but just because I'm screaming doesn't mean I'm screaming out of anger, I could be screaming out of passion or frustration. I've always said our songs aren't angry songs, they're just passionate, and if some people can't hack it, that's OK, they don't have to listen to them.

A male journalist once criticised me for calling women cunts in one of my songs. But if anyone can say it, I can! I have one! I can say whatever I want, I'm not interested in being politically correct at all. It's boring, it's dishonest and it's conformist. I want to live my life to the fullest and push borders. I don't want to even have borders! I don't always want to be saying the right thing.

I didn't even think about being a woman until I started getting interviewed. Seriously, they'd ask things like 'What does it feel like to be a woman in a band and isn't this a man's world?' and I would go 'Well, I don't know where you've been but where I come from, the space in my head is not like that, it doesn't look like that!' It's not as bad in America, those kind of questions mostly get asked in England. You just want to say 'Get over it!' What's the big deal? It's so irritating, it's sort of an insult. 'Can you work as hard as the guys?' What? Better! Yeah, it's an insult!

I have never felt unequal to men. If anything I felt stronger than them, it was just the way I grew up. I always thought I was a tomboy and I've always thought I was probably bisexual somewhere inside of me.

I read this book about Billie Holiday once and I remember thinking that she felt exactly the way I do and they were asking her the same dumb questions back then as they are now! And how many years ago was that? Fifty? It's bullshit!

I think women do take things out on themselves more than men. It's like a martyr syndrome. I've done it before, I'm sure that's why I have an ulcer. My stomach's been hurting since the age of three. My whole life my dad was saying 'Quit bellyaching'. I literally complain about my stomach constantly. I went to the doctor's and he told me I have a really bad ulcer. Well, it figured. People think you're complaining for nothing. I knew there was something wrong, especially when I threw up blood into the toilet. I stopped drinking for three months straight.

I started drinking when I was about 13 because I was really introverted and I think it extroverted me a bit. When I first moved to Minneapolis I had bottles of Jim Beam and Jack Daniels by my bed at all times. I was a fully-fledged alcoholic, drinking as soon as I woke up. I guess I wasn't very happy. These days when I'm at home with my husband, I'm happy and I don't drink as much, he doesn't really like to drink. But when I'm away from him it's bad. I need to drink. If I start thinking too much I don't like it. Reality's too sharp and grey and you can hear everything people are saying. It's usually something stupid about the way you look and it's so annoying.

I tend to write when I'm depressed or angry because if I'm happy, I'm just having a good time. I don't know how people can write happy music. I like sad music, it makes me feel better, more alive I guess. I like tortured people, people like Leonard Cohen, Nick Cave and Billie Holiday. I can relate to them more and I'm sure it's because I grew up more or less in isolation with an abusive stepmother.

People say I should have therapy—but no way! I don't like the idea of it at all. It irons you out and who says you're supposed to be a certain way anyway? It scares me, it's like people thinking they can brainwash you or something! I can therapise myself! Singing really makes me feel better, and making records. It's weird, when you think about what drives you, you can't even figure it out. It's like you have to do it but sometimes you don't want to and you hate it!

My songs are really personal but a lot of the time I shroud the meanings on purpose. I write in metaphors and symbolism and double meanings and get them all tangled up, so you have to be at least into it or clever enough to untangle it. A lot of them are codes for things and if people can figure them out I'm really impressed!

Some of my songwriting is really automatic and I'm not sure where it's coming from, but all of a sudden I get this feeling like I have to grab a notebook. It's a physical feeling. I seem to have this huge brain diary and then it all comes out and I read it back and I think, what the fuck! Sometimes I don't even know what I'm doing. I think writing's a way of solving your problems and maybe even your future problems. It's like your subconscious is writing and telling your conscious what's wrong. It's really interesting. Some of it's like that, and then some of it's from ideas in my mind, or I'm pissed off with a certain person.

I think mainly I write about my nightmares. I don't like to talk about it too much, it's a bit like magic, you're not supposed to talk about it. Lori has a lot of prediction dreams. It's amazing, me and her can basically read each other's minds now. We do it all the time. It's probably from being around each other so much, but there are energies there, they're just not tapped into very much. I swear women are better at it than men though, that's why there's more women psychics. Maybe it's to do with intuition, I don't know.

I'm really obsessed with babies and angels too and I'm sure it's to do with my dreams. I collect all kinds of baby and angel things although I'm not maternal at all. Maybe it's to do with the whole birth thing, with a woman being like a universe in herself. Well, that's how I think of the universe, like someone's huge womb. I don't know, I have weird thoughts in my head!

I like magicky things too. It's probably to do with stuff I liked as a kid. When I was a kid I was way into glass figurines and I was thinking about them once, and I realised that I dress like those figurines! I'd always play with them when I was grounded because I never had Barbie dolls or regular toys. I had these antique figurines and I would make believe with them all the time. They were my friends. So I probably just turned into my imagination because I played with those things for so long. But it is weird when you look at yourself and you think oh my God, I've turned into a glass doll!

I guess I started wearing old dresses when I turned about 17. I started dyeing my hair and fucking around. I always fucked around with my clothes anyway, but I started getting into old dresses mainly when I went to Portland because they had some really good stores there.

I hate the press for scrutinising my clothes though, I just like certain styles, and old shoes, and I can't help it. I guess clothes are a form of expression and sometimes I wear things because they're just comfortable. I can't wear long things on stage because I can't move my legs, I feel trapped. I did it the other night and it was horrible. I couldn't sing right or anything! It was like being in a straitjacket or something. It's like Lori can't wear long sleeves and she has to drum barefoot, she has to feel the pedals. If you're wearing something that's not you, it's just too weird!

You know what really pisses me off? When the press say I dress like a baby. I'm sorry, but a baby wouldn't fit into my dresses! It probably has more to do with my personality and when I wear these dresses, it just comes out. I mean I feel like if I go into a room of people, they have to be 13 for me to feel like they're younger than me. I'm 30, so they're usually not older than me but I always think they are. Age is pretty weird!

Another thing the press have said is that I'll probably calm down now I'm married. Well, they haven't met my husband! When you meet someone, they don't tame you, they make you feel more content and just in love basically. People are always trying to get around the fact that I got married, because it isn't very rock'n'roll, is it?

One journalist asked me if I'd got married because Courtney and Kurt did, and he was serious! I couldn't really believe it!

Credentials

Band:	Babes In Toyland
Signed to:	Southern Records in Britain, Warners in America.
Managed by:	Richard Bishop

Past bands:	The Neurotics, The Venarays, Sugar Baby Doll
Select discography:	*Spanking Machine* LP (1990)
	To Mother LP (1991)
	Fontanelle LP (1992)
	Painkillers LP (1993)
Other projects:	*Crunt* LP (1993, Trance Syndicate Records) with her husband, Stuart Gray.

Björk

'*If* you had a woman who was the equivalent of Woody Allen, charming, brilliant and with her own personality, she'd be nowhere.'

Björk

▼

Defying all known forms of convenient categorisation, Björk Gudmundsdottir has forged herself a highly individual style both visually and musically. Crashing through the indie rock ceiling which sheltered her previous band, the Sugarcubes, Björk has come to celebrate female sensuality with an unfettered passion for all kinds of music. Her peculiar voice possesses a sense of freedom, racing through a range of emotion with songs which draw on universal symbols for meaning and space. She has a truly inspiring belief in individual expression and an irrepressible spirit, and has attracted the music and fashion media who have leapt on her unique originality with enthusiasm, although too often their treatment has been disturbingly patronising.

Coming from Iceland, where she grew up in a hippy community with her unorthodox mother, Björk put her faith in individuality right from the start. In such an under-populated land, people who refuse to conform stand out remarkably, and from an early age Björk was aware of her difference from other children, so she immersed herself in her own activities, singing songs.

From the age of 6 until she was 14, Björk learnt to play the flute and the piano at a local music school, and impressed her teachers so much with her singing that they introduced her to Iceland's only national radio station. In turn this led to a recording contract, and in 1977, when she was just 11, Björk released her debut album, *Björk*.

When punk arrived, Björk immersed herself in the new energy, and began forming bands from the age of 13. Exodus and Jam 80 were relatively short lived, Tappi Tikarrass (roughly translated as 'Cork the Bitch's Ass'!) released two albums as did Kukl, (meaning 'Sorcery') who also caused a national scandal when they appeared on Icelandic television with a scantily-clad, eight-months pregnant Björk.

In 1986, Kukl's anarcho-punk activism gave way to the mischief of the Sugarcubes, when Björk, together with Einar Orn and Siggi Baldursson, left to start a new band with Thor Eldon (Björk's one-time husband and father of her son Sindri), Magga Ornolfsdottir and Bragi Olafsson. None of them had ambition, they were fun-seekers looking to subvert with a sense of naughtiness, but instead they achieved international success. Their distinctive style and in particular Björk's strange and haunting vocal caught the imagination of the music press in 1987 when they released the first of three albums, *Life's Too Good*, and over the next six years The Sugarcubes evolved into a much more serious concern.

Eventually Björk decided she had to do something for herself and split to embark on a solo career, leaving the other Sugarcubes to follow suit, although not quite so successfully. Having been involved with a wide variety of musical collaborations, including big band, dance, free-form rock jazz and death metal projects, as well as Tappi Tikarrass, Kukl and the Sugarcubes, Björk had more than earned the record deal which gave her absolute artistic control, and launched herself into the making of *Debut*, the album which was to introduce her to a much wider and more varied audience.

Since the release of *Debut* in 1993, Björk has become an icon of visual as well as musical style. Her penchant for second-hand clothing has been transformed into eco-friendly fashion spreads for magazines and Sunday supplements, and her witty hair-knots have been widely copied. She has also been condescendingly described as a 'pixie woman' with 'elfin' charm, a 'child woman' and an 'exotic' beauty, all of which have understandably annoyed her. Fully aware of the imperialistic attitudes which greeted the Sugarcubes, especially in Britain, Björk believes that the media's ethereal imaginings of her are simply an extension of this. She puts it down to a kind of ignorant fantasy people entertain about Iceland's relatively unexplored culture, which, though rich in mythology, is hardly a land of trolls and polar bears.

More than anything though, Björk is angry about the lack of freedom for women to develop as characters rather than physically desirable beings. While men are judged in terms of their intellect, imagination and wit, women tend to be looked at as little more than bodies, particularly when they're involved in entertainment. Björk has clung fiercely to her own convictions, irrespective of conservative standards, using the opportunities afforded to her by the likes of Italian *Vogue* to play with ideas of female imagery, and has proved that women do not need to cramp their style in order to be successful. She has refused to compromise herself artistically or personally, implicitly trusting in her passions, sensual understanding and playful sense of humour to show that female individuality owes as much to attitude as it does to looks. And while most of the world is still some way off from ingesting this invaluable lesson, Björk's infectious confidence in her convictions makes her example impossible to ignore.

Björk

I lived by the sea in Iceland, and it does affect you a lot. I went there for Christmas last year and got drunk with my friends, and we were discussing the affect the place has on you. Several of them were forced to move abroad, like myself. I've lived in England for a year now and I thought I would never, ever have to do that.

It's strange because it's too small to be able to work there and it's too big to be able to carry the world around with you. So my friends and I were laughing because there's this endless 'can't live with, can't live without' situation for people like me. One of my friends is a sculptor and another is a painter and if you're doing something like that, Iceland is no place for you. It feeds you 100 per cent when it comes to inspiration and when it comes to self-identity, and when I go there my batteries just completely fill up in one day. It's not a coincidence. But when it comes to actually getting it out of your system, that's when there are problems, because people there are lovely, but it's just too small a population to make them get what you're on about. I'm doing fine there now, but the only reason is because I've got recognition abroad. They fall for that, the people.

I haven't really adapted to England. I'm a visitor here and I always will be, and that's another thing I have a laugh about with my friends when we're drinking together—that we will always be visitors. It's a joke! All of them who go abroad to study, they always come back, and it doesn't matter if they get hilarious, outrageous job offers. They'd rather go back home and work in a shop! It's such a different energy there.

In Iceland you're either normal, and you do a normal job and you do everything in a normal way, or you're a weirdo, the town freak. It's as big as England, but it's only got the same population as London's Edgware Road, and it's very beautiful, but it's a small society, so everybody is watching each other. If the dentist's wife starts going out with the shoemaker, everybody knows, and either you get completely obsessed with all that, or you don't give a shit. There's no, what do you call it, in between. So when my mother, who was single, had me, it was a scandal because she didn't want to be a housewife. She didn't want to wear make up, she wanted to let her hair hang down and wear her eccentric clothes and she was just an outcast.

My parents had me when they were very young. My mother was 19 and my father was 20. They had been together since they were 14 and 15. They split up when I was one year old.

My dad's family were very, very conservative. The men were men and the women were women, and if you fell in love with someone else while you were married, you just forgot about it. You did your duty, loved your husband and your kids and shut up. And it was the same for men, just work, love your wife and shut up. My mother was completely the opposite. She'd listen to her heart and forget her duties, which got a bit mad sometimes, because she'd forget to bring me up. But I could see both ways, and pick from each. There was the organisation and the discipline, and the going to work, even if you didn't feel like it, but at the end of the day what mattered was your heart—and all that hippy freedom shit!

A lot of people, including my relatives, would say my mum was mad, because she didn't bring me up properly, but I was fine. From the age of four or five, I had to manage myself, and it wasn't a problem. I would wake myself up, get dressed, get the bus and go to school. I think it was very healthy because I couldn't rely on anyone else.

I remember deciding when I was about five that I'd either do things my way and have a lot of fun or I'd do things other people's way and be a doormat. Once I decided I wanted to do something–I can't remember what–and the rest of the kids in the street didn't. I could sense a certain 'Well, you just don't do that!' So I made a decision that I wouldn't give a shit about them.

People have always found me strange and it just makes me laugh you know. I guess it's a kind of handicap, for people not to be able to understand you, but I'm not really bothered because I have a good group of friends and to them I'm the most down-to-earth, common sense person you could ever find. And I think I am a very no-bull-shit, straightforward kind of person. I guess it's a compliment to be considered complicated!

Where I grew up, there was 24-hour music and there was always a queue of hippies waiting for the record player. The first time I made an independent decision to play a record, it was Sparks' 'Kimono My House', and I was seven or eight. When it was my turn they fucking had to listen to it, and I would play it all the time! They didn't like it, they thought it was too poppy, but Sparks were really comical. I was really into them for two years until the singer said there were two things in the world that he didn't like, animals and children, and that really hurt me.

The first record I learnt by heart was *The Sound of Music* when I was three or four. And then there were all the records my mother played–The Beatles, Joni Mitchell and Jimi Hendrix. But the music that fascinated me was usually instrumental. I've never been that mad about singers. I never really considered myself a singer until lately. My heart has always been in the music, the instruments. I tried to learn the flute but I didn't have the patience and that's probably the reason why I ended up a singer because I didn't have the patience to tackle any instrument.

What I really like to do is write songs with other people my age, and get really involved together and mix personalities. It's like a musical love affair, over-emotional madness! That's what turns me on and I happen to sing because that's my tool.

When I tell people I've been writing songs since I was very little, they look at me as if I was Mozart, but it's not at all like that. It wasn't like they were masterpieces. It was just very natural for me as a kid to write songs. I don't know, things like, 'I have to go to the shop, I have to go to the shop, I hope I won't forget what I'm supposed to buy'. You know, those kind of songs. And I would spend a lot of time on my own, being an only child, and have great fun just making little songs. It wasn't exactly 'Bohemian Rhapsody', they were very simple.

I think for every situation there's a song. I used to terrify my friends because I always had a little ghetto blaster and pockets full of tapes, and I'd sit in the background, because we would always be together, and I'd play a song. And then we'd change the subject and I'd play another song, and then we'd walk down the street and it would start raining and I'd put on another song. I'd try to change the song to fit what people were talking about. It would get really sentimental or really hardcore or whatever. That's what music is really all about. I don't think music is so much about what it's become, because it's kind of like, become a monument.

Truly, music is just feelings and I'm not trying to be philosophical or anything. That is the beauty of music, that it's just down to earth and about really boring things like driving your car or taking the tube or doing an interview or anything. All those things, that's what music should be. It's gone wrong because of a combination of things. I've been taking part in it with my record, *Debut*, and I'm trying to fight it. Although I'm not bitter about it, because you can't really point out what it is that's going wrong, if it's the interviews or the photo shoots or the videos or the record companies or whatever. At the end of the day the only thing that can be right or wrong is the attitude. People can be on the biggest record label in the world and do 97 videos and you can still sense what they actually are like and if they're writing songs that matter.

Obviously you can make music for so many different reasons. One of my favourite artists is Madonna and she's not doing it for musical reasons, she wants to change the world! And fair enough. I think if music existed as a person, music would be proud that Madonna actually uses music to do that.

When I write tunes, they're more about the foreplay than the intercourse, because as a true female, I guess that's what I'm more interested in! I'd rather play with my imagination and flirt more with my head. If I meet a person who's wearing clothes that hide their body, but they have a mad, corrupted mind and really tease me, I find that much more exciting than someone with the most perfect body in the world, who says nothing to turn me on.

It's also a question of foreplay—to what? It could be foreplay to taking an aeroplane to Thailand, or a build-up to meeting a friend or buying your first car. All those things are a real turn-on. I find it very difficult to draw a line between what's sex and what isn't. It can be very, very sexy to drive a car, and completely unsexy to flirt with someone at a bar. At the end of the day, it's all about foreplay and climax. As humans that's how we do everything, whether it's writing a book or running a country. It's all done with that kind of energy.

I was 11 when I made my first album. My stepfather was in a band and he played Jimi Hendrix kind of stuff. I was brought up with him from the age of four. I can't remember how it developed, but I was one of those kids who'd be singing all the time. Not showing off, just singing to myself, and my dad knew people who were in the music business and they knew I could sing. I guess it was also the right time in Iceland for a child star. They asked my mum if I'd be into it and my mum was right into it, and convinced me to do it. I got to pick the songs myself, I wrote one of the songs, and it was a brilliant opportunity for me to see a studio and how it works and the magic things that are done there. And it became really big in Iceland, it went platinum. And my mum wanted me to do another one but I didn't want to. There was a lot of pressure on me but by that time I'd been introduced to the goods, because I'd been in a classical music school since I was five and I was really frustrated because I had passion for music, but playing Bach and Beethoven just bored me to death. To realise that you could go and pick up any instrument you wanted and write a tune was just brilliant!

When I was a teenager I'd go to this little sailor bar with several of my girlfriends and one of us would seduce the DJ and get him really drunk so we could get in the booth with our own records! Even now I'm awful when I get drunk, especially when I get really drunk. I'm right up there wanting to hear my favourite tunes all in a row, forever!

I would always be the one who would hang out in the record shops and kind of know what was going on. If it was somebody's wedding or someone was putting on a fashion show, they'd ask me to play records because I had a big collection.

I've been in bands ever since I was 12 and I've always been in two or three at a time, because I wanted to play with all the mad people in Iceland, to experience everything. When I was about 14, I was in an all-girl punk band, and a punk band that played poppy tunes called Tappi Tikarrass. Well, let's call it happy punk, that probably sorts it out. Tappi Tikarrass actually did quite well in Iceland and then I got bored with it and I started Kukl, a jazz-punk band. When we played abroad we were always compared to Rip Rig and Panic although we didn't know about them. They were supposed to be some sort of jazz punk. There were thousands of others but I won't even go into it, it'll just complicate things.

I guess Kukl were kind of in the punk intelligentsia, although I shouldn't say that myself. It's like blowing my own trumpet, but I guess it's the truth. We formed a little company and put out records and held a lot of poetry readings and exhibitions and made films, and we were very productive and the band was almost like a secondary thing for us. All the people in Iceland who were getting bored to death who wanted to put things out, decided to just do it, and sell 100 copies of whatever it was, because there were so few people in Iceland and there wasn't any money to do anything.

I went on the telly with Kukl when I was pregnant, and at the time Madonna was really big with 'Like A Virgin'. We kind of took the piss because we got a lot of pressure on us as we weren't commercial enough. All the media hated us from day one, and it wasn't until the Sugarcubes got recognition abroad that they swallowed everything they'd said before. There was a lot of hypocrisy. But anyway I decided to wear just a bra and a skirt underneath my pregnant belly to take the piss out of Madonna, who at that point was the stereotype of all the crap music that was around. We just thought it was very funny that a very pregnant woman would do that. And basically it was a scandal in Iceland and I got almost sued by a 60-year-old woman. Her mother, who was 90, watched the programme and had a heart attack! She actually survived, but for people who don't know the scene in Iceland it's hard to explain that that's how self-contained it is.

When I was in the Sugarcubes we were just obsessed with that society, and changing it, and shocking it and provoking it and teasing it and we were having a great time. We didn't want to go abroad at all, and we said no for two years. When we did go it was strange, because of course the Sugarcubes were misunderstood from day one. And we wanted to be in a way, but in a different way to the way we were.

In Iceland we'd stuck together through thick and thin as a gang of people for eight years and had quite a colourful past, and then some bigheaded journalist from *Melody Maker* decided that we were his pet of the month. The arrogance in the British press, that kind of 'We discovered you so shut up and behave', just didn't go down very well with us because we had a past in a country which they thought was full of Eskimos and polar bears. I mean, there's not one polar bear or Eskimo in Iceland! They were so full of ignorance. They weren't really interested in trying to find out anything about us. They thought we were ethereal puffin eaters even though we would say very down-to-earth, solid things.

All this 'Elfin woman, Pixie woman' stuff I get now is some kind of leftover from that. Because they decided beforehand, with this imperialistic view of theirs, that we were some sort of exotic property from another galaxy. And they couldn't deal with the fact that we were six different individuals who ran our own record company and radio station in Iceland, who managed ourselves all the way through, and who put out a magazine.

I'm not bitter about it because in a way that's what I've always thrived on. In Iceland I survived because I was looked on as someone who was different. Going abroad and being looked on as different again kept me surviving.

When I broke away from the Sugarcubes, I didn't feel scared because in Iceland I was always doing lots of projects and working with other bands as an individual. To work on my own was not scary. What was scary was to allow myself to be selfish, because all the things that I've done in the past have always been for other people or purposes, whether it was writing a lyric or doing a video that suited the Sugarcubes, or writing a backing vocal to suit another artist or the music to suit a film. What is difficult for me now, is suddenly to suit myself. It's not really in my character. Well it is, I mean everybody's got it I guess, but I kind of have to look for it really hard and I tend to forget about it and I rather ignore it.

I'm not worried about actually doing it, because I'm a housewife and I'm quite used to getting everybody together and sorting them out, but to focus it all on me is weird, because I get scared of being boring. And all the media attention I've had with *Debut* has complicated things. I'm just repeating myself and I'd love it if I could talk about something else. If I was a scientist I could talk about diseases or something! That's why I mention David Attenborough a lot in my interviews, because he's always talking about animals, do you know what I mean?

I mean I am very proud of the attention I've had as well. I've felt very honoured at times. And I can't imagine that someone wouldn't be if Italian *Vogue* offered to do 12 pages on them! But after a while you get the feeling that they're misunderstanding something, and they're expecting something you can't give, because it isn't in you.

I think a lot of the attention I've had from the fashion press has been to do with being the right person at the right time. There was just a space in the English media that needed to be filled. Everybody has been into recycling and green issues, and I was wearing second-hand clothes, and making new things out of old things, which I've been doing for 15 years, so it was no accident.

I've had a certain clothes sense since I was 12. It comes from a lack of good clothes shops in Iceland! I would go to second-hand shops because I always spent my money on records, and because it was more creative and a lot more fun than going to your average Miss Selfridge type place. When I was 13 or 14, I was wearing tiny little dresses with big boots, and I just thought it was funny. I've always liked to have a sense of humour in the way I dress, which is probably very anti-stylish, because being stylish is all about being very serious.

I like to have fun with everything, it's not just clothes. It doesn't matter what it is, I like to do everything with passion, whether it's driving a car, or choosing a restaurant, or where to go on holiday. I think everybody knows what they like.

There is definitely an element of escape involved. I want new things everyday, and I guess early on I decided to make an advantage of that. If you listen to all the records I've been on in Iceland, you can really hear it. One month I'm playing jazz with a lot of people, six months later I'm working completely alone with computers and synthesizers, and then I'm a vocalist in a band, and next I'm in charge. So it is about escape, but at the same time, if I look back, there is a certain continuity to it. I move on and I learn.

This year I've learnt really fast, to face the responsibility of being the person who asks for things, because it's very easy to give. Ridiculous as it sounds, once you start taking and saying 'No I want that!' it becomes like a one-way street, you become a spoilt kid. But if you are the one who's giving all the time, you just automatically get things back. If you love somebody very much, you just feed off that somehow, but if you reverse that circulation you become a greedy bastard who's never fed.

I know all these things sound very sickly and very housewifey, but I guess that's what I function on. But it's funny, this year I could definitely feel some macho vibes happening! I said all my life it doesn't matter if you're a girl or a boy. Fuck all that shit, it's just people making a big thing out of nothing at the end of the day! But I've definitely felt this year with being my own boss that certain things have been linked with men and it's not a coincidence.

What really pisses me off is not being dealt with by people on an equal level. I'm a housewife from Iceland and I like to write and sing songs. You either like it or you don't. But it gets blurred and changed into something it's not, it pisses me off. Women are just not allowed to be characters. A man is allowed to be scruffy or a hunk, or a Woody Allen or an Albert Einstein, and still be accepted as 100 per cent man. But if a woman hasn't got a certain figure or doesn't make an effort to remain on a level which is considered feminine, she isn't in the game.

If you had a woman who was the equivalent of Woody Allen, charming, brilliant and with her own personality, she'd be nowhere. That pisses me off more than being dismissed as an Eskimo or whatever, because if I had to pick between the hunk and Woody Allen, I'd say I was more in the Woody Allen category!

Still, with music you can express yourself and you can do so many things. I guess I'll stick with it, but I am terrified of plans. Plans are the biggest turn-off for me. The minute something is decided I just freak out! I like to live my life like the line in my song 'Big Time Sensuality'—'I don't know my future after this weekend, And I don't want to!' Of course when you've got a kid and things going on, you have to make some plans, but when you ask me about the future, I would like to take it as it comes and see what happens. And that takes the most effort!

Credentials

Signed to:	One Little Indian Records
Managed by:	Derek Birket
Select past bands:	Exodus
	Tappi Tikarrass
	Kukl
	Sugarcubes
Select discography:	Sugarcubes—
	Life's Too Good LP (1988)
	Here Today, Tomorrow, Next Week LP (1989)
	Stick Around for Joy LP (1992)
	It's It LP (1992)
	Björk—
	Debut LP (1993)
	'Human Behaviour' single—various mixes available (1993)
	'Big Time Sensuality' single—various mixes available (1993)

Tanya Donelly

'*I*f women could learn to be as unattractive as men, it would go a long way towards demystifying females in bands.'

Tanya Donelly

▼

Once she found the confidence to step out of the band she'd shared with her best friend for several years, Tanya Donelly freed herself into an expression she'd previously resisted. With her own band, Belly, she has relaxed into songwriting, drawing on her traditional sensibilities without feeling the need for spiking them into a context which isn't wholly her own. Her debut album *Star* shimmers with delicious melodies and fairy-tale imagery, bringing an essentially female sensuality into play, yet at the same time, much to Donelly's irritation, has inspired all manner of absurd male fantasies about the 'sweet little' figure at its centre.

Raised in a hippy environment in the tiny state of Rhode Island on America's east coast, Donelly was traumatised by human contact as a child. She constantly threw up in school where she felt alienated, until she met Kristin Hersh who was later to become her step sister. Together the girls formed a barrier against the outside world, losing themselves in music. They taught themselves to play guitar and eventually formed Throwing Muses who went on to become one of the best bands on the indie/college rock scene. Their haunting songs jarred and flowed, characterised by Hersh's unmistakable voice, thriving on the images which forced their way out of her during a ten-year period, as she suffered from a form of schizophrenia known as bi-polarity. Donelly delivered a couple of

95

compositions for each album, until finally she felt the need to branch out on her own.

Initially the guitarist blew off some steam with The Breeders, a side project she developed with Kim Deal of The Pixies and Josephine Wiggs of The Perfect Disaster. They recorded an album, *Pod*, which gave Donelly the confidence she needed to leave the Muses, and by the time The Breeders came to their second release, *Safari*, she'd left them and had begun developing Belly.

As the only girl in a band with three boys, Donelly started out feeling uncomfortable as Belly's frontwoman. She realised that she'd been treated like a doll instead of the powerfully imaginative and creative force she really is. When her first bass player, Fred Abong, left, she recruited another woman to deflect her situation, and found Gail Greenwood, a 32-year-old fireball of energy, whose exuberant stage antics shocked Belly's audience.

Now one of America and Britain's most respected and popular guitar bands, Belly have seen their debut album turn gold and enjoy front-cover status from the music press. Donelly continues to feel patronised though and is angered by the emphasis placed on her little frame and bubbly laughter which has even encouraged other women to attack her for being some kind of gender traitor. The common portrayal of her as fragile and giggly is hugely inaccurate and belies her articulate intelligence and formidable talent.

Donelly's struggle to be accepted as a sexual, emotional human being who doesn't exist on a pedestal veiled in mystery will continue until people stop making judgments about women's bodies and start realising that no one needs big hands to play the guitar. Her strengths deserve to be recognised without the weakening taint of false romanticism. Then perhaps she will be seen as flesh and blood, not porcelain.

Tanya Donelly

For the first four years of my life I moved around a lot with my family, driving between Rhode Island and California. But my father couldn't get work in San Francisco so we came home to settle.

People came and went at our house all the time, although it wasn't a commune exactly, it was our house. My parents get really upset if I talk about it in realistic terms sometimes and there were good things about it, I was exposed to things that I think were good for me as a person, although probably nothing that I'd want my children to be exposed to. There was a lot of nudity, a lot of drugs and a lot of very strange situations although I have to stress that my parents were very good parents, they were very loving and support-ive and good to us, but I have been left with a lot of images that I wish that I didn't have, pictures that won't go away. I do use them in songs, I think if I didn't have music as an outlet I would definitely be in therapy but that sounds really typical and I don't like to use it. I have a really hard time with people who present their resume of scars, I don't like it, it's really cheap, so I'm lucky in the way that I have something that I can put a lot into.

My parents had rejected the hippy lifestyle as I got older, and I think a lot of the precepts of the late 1960s and early 1970s were based on just bullshit, concepts that don't exist. I don't think open relationships are part of human nature, I don't think open marriages have anything to do with human nature, I don't think that drugs expand your consciousness. I think those things are dangerous and corrosive and a lot of concepts from that time were really so corroding. And most of the people that I was exposed to then were just lying. It was just an image thing. There were great things about it too. Obviously the political awareness was crucial and it still permeates the way people think in this country now, and I think that was an extremely necessary thing to happen, but I think that was the only good thing to come out of it. And the music of course!

I met Kristin in school. We're step-sisters, there's no blood between us. Both of our parents were married at the time we met but in time her parents divorced and my parents divorced and eventually my father married her mother. They knew each other through us but marriage was a bad idea!

It wasn't embarrassing but it kind of forced a relationship on us that wasn't part of our friendship. In some ways it was really good because we got to spend a lot of time together and share a room and things like that, but because our parents ended up with such a strange tension between them, a tension developed between us that I wish hadn't had to happen. They were happy for a while and those years were good but then it started to get chaotic.

It was a bad situation because we moved into the house where Kristin had been raised, and her father moved out. It's hard not to choose sides, but we kept it out of our relationship as much as possible, we hardly ever talked about it. Until they got divorced we never had a real conversation about their marriage, but as soon as we left the house we left that behind. But it was difficult to maintain the best friendship and the sister thing. Sisterhood I'm convinced is the most complicated relationship in the world!

Neither of us liked school. We were really geeky and awkward and creepy. It was really weird. First of all I was so scared of everyone that I could barely function. I don't know why. I used to throw up every single day before I went to school and then again when I got to school, so my desk was separated from the rest of the class.

I don't know what I was afraid of. It was probably just human contact because I'd been raised in this community of people that didn't involve a lot of other children and my parents were never real authority figures, so real school was my first taste of that.

To begin with I went to this kind of hippy kindergarten called The Pink Pussycat which was full of children who'd been raised the way I'd been raised, and so that wasn't too dramatic for me. But then we moved to Newport and at that point I was exposed to other children who I didn't have anything in common with lifestyle-wise and also it was my first experience with authority, the first time I experienced an adult being strict and stern. I didn't understand the behaviour of anybody in that situation. I felt like I was from France or something! I didn't know the code, I didn't understand what the rules were. So me and Kristin kind of gravitated towards each other and I mean it was the best thing that ever happened to me, but we definitely reinforced each other's separateness too. And we also developed this thing which we never verbalised but we decided everyone hated us because we were special!

When I was 12 I was involved in a car accident in which my mother and I came very close to death and at the time the family had a friend who was very into Krishna. He started to sort of take me over in a way and I was very, very vulnerable at that point. It did change my life and it's a young age for this to happen, but I became absolutely obsessed with the concept of God. And I still am to this day, it's the passion of my life. I've always had a real visceral sense of God but I've never had a specific sense and I'm getting to the point where I don't need a specific, where I feel like that's not necessary, that you don't need to pray in order to live your life well but at that point in my life I'd had this thing happen to me and I wanted to live well and I wanted to find out what that meant.

It's something where only now I feel comfortable even using the word God because it's such a loaded word, but there isn't any other. I don't want to make a word up and I don't want to avoid using it just to avoid being embarrassed. It has a negative connotation. My parents were both atheists when I was growing up and my grandparents on my mother's side were both atheists so I don't have any spiritual or religious background, so I guess I'm lucky in a way but I do have to be careful how I use the word because I don't want to be misconstrued. I don't have any image that goes with it, I don't have a male image in my head, but it does unfortunately carry that.

When we were 15, Kristin and I founded Throwing Muses with this girl named Elaine who had started to play music with us. Music was something we'd always been exposed to. We'd always been music fans, and we have our birthdays right next to each other and one year—I think it was when we were 14—Kristin's father gave her a guitar and my father gave me one and we just started playing. We played along with a Beatles songbook for a while, but all the chords were wrong in the book, so we ended up playing really weird chords! We ended up wanting to write our own things. And Kristin's father actually writes songs so we'd play along with his songs, and it just seemed like it was the kind of thing we could do. Nobody presented any opposition to it. And nobody even seemed surprised or in the least bit impressed that we were doing it so it just felt natural.

We were really slow as far as the boy thing goes. I was less slow, I always had crushes and stuff but it never occurred to us that we would do anything like date until we were 17. We were 17 when we first started even allowing the concept of dating into our heads! Everyone around us was consumed by it, our peers and schoolmates and it seemed like a waste of energy. It still does!

Feeling ugly definitely had something to do with not getting into boys too. That's what I mean by watching a lot of girls my age get distracted by it—boys would become their mirrors and especially at that age it's much easier to do, whereas our guitars were our mirrors. It sounds so dumb but the fact that we felt physically worthless was a real blessing. Wretched is the word Kristin likes to use—we were wretched!

I don't think you ever lose that feeling of ugliness once you've had it. I feel better now than I ever have as far as my worth goes but still, especially when I'm at the beginning of a relationship, when I'm first in contact with people, I tend to get almost angry with them in a way because they're too stupid to see that I'm awful! It's like I'm just waiting for them to go 'Oh No!' I think that kind of awkwardness never goes away and it can be triggered off by something really small, like if you knock something over or if there's a faux pas in a social situation it just immediately comes right back! I get angry with myself for not being able to overcome that stuff fully and it makes me feel developmentally retarded in some ways, you know. But I think that there are a million ages that you're always stuck at, and that's the sharpest one.

Something that I have a hard time with is when you've set the tone of a relationship with people and it's really hard to break out of. Once the mood has been set in a situation I never feel that I can get past that. Once an impression has been made or a mould has been made or whatever, I can't get through it. I think, well today I'm going to go in and I'm going to really be me and they're going to see me, but it doesn't work like that!

I know people who are very much in control of their lives and are also incredibly productive so it's a hard call saying that being out of control makes you more creative. I think that loneliness just very simply equals time, like if you have a lonely childhood or a lonely young adulthood then you have a lot more time than someone who hasn't been lonely, and you have that much more time to work on yourself even though it doesn't feel like that at the time. There's a lot more introspection and more reaching out and grabbing things from the outside world and pulling them in that goes on when you're lonely. You watch more. You have time not friends!

I still have that fear of people that I've always had and I don't know what it is. It always takes a really long time to get to know me, which is weird because I've always been more outgoing than Kristin, although she's always been more honestly friendly. That makes me sound like a bad person, but I tend to want to smooth any situation over and sometimes that can make people think they have more access to me than they actually do have. It's my own fault because I set things up in that way. I don't mean so much in a one-to-one situation, more in a band situation when you're surrounded by people. I'm willing to let it get to a certain point and I'm like that with my songs as well because there's always a handful of people who want something from me and it frightens me. And unfortunately it makes me think about how I'm going to write my next batch of songs. Like, well all right, that one was a bit too open, so how about this? See, this song doesn't mean anything!

I might be giving myself too much credit, but I think people saw my songs as not having too much depth in Throwing Muses because of the context in which they were aired. I was in a band that was very weighty and so in contrast to Kristin's songs, mine seemed lighter.

I'm not interested in revealing myself in songs. Kristin writes so much more from within than I do. She doesn't see what she does as self-expression, because she doesn't see the things she writes about as being specific to her, they're more universal. But I'm more guarded.

My songwriting never became an issue until the very end of my being in Throwing Muses. I was the lead guitar player and that's how I thought of myself. But around the time of *Hunkpapa*, the second to last album I did with the band, I started to relax about the fact that I had more traditional songwriting sensibilities than Kristin did. It used to make me feel very daunted because it was so easy and I always thought it should be harder. I thought I shouldn't be happy with something simple, because it was easy for me to leave a song in a simple state, so I would throw things in to skew them a little bit, to make them more in keeping with Kristin's style. But around the time of *Hunkpapa*, I started to go 'Well, this is the way I do it—there are three chords in this song and that's the way it stays!'

Towards the end of my being in Throwing Muses I felt frustrated, but not resentful. Any tension about it lasted for such a short time, because I left before it could become a real issue. To be fair to Kristin, it was her band, and just because I was suddenly starting to have a wet spell or whatever didn't mean that the formula of her band should change.

The week just before I actually left Throwing Muses was scary because the concept of bringing it up was bad. I knew once it was on the table it could be dealt with, but I have a really hard time with first words. I had a whole, very gentle, easing out of the water speech prepared, but I ended up knocking on Kristin's door and crying the minute she opened it. I think she thought I was going to tell her I had cancer or something. But once it was out, she and I were both fine. It was everybody else around the band who freaked!

It was sad on a personal level because I hadn't spent a day away from her since I was eight years old and I do miss her, but it's never going to reach the point where we won't know what to say to each other and that's a security blanket for me. I mean when we're together, we're seven again!

I think we just got to the point where musically we weren't good for each other anymore. We were stagnating. The guy who produced our last album together, *The Real Ramona*, said that the atmosphere was musical when I was in the studio on my own, and when Kristin was in there alone, but when we in there together it was just dead water.

Playing with The Breeders was really good for me as a guitar player, because it let me know that I was capable of playing outside the Muses microcosm. Originally I started The Breeders as a side project with Kim Deal, who was then in The Pixies, and Josephine Wiggs who was in Perfect Disaster. It was the first time I'd played with anyone else and it was really good for me to know that I could play with other people!

Kim was a completely different person when I first met her. The first time I ever saw The Pixies play, Kim had come straight from work where she was a secretary in a doctor's office and she had this ruffly blouse on and this black skirt and pumps and the most insane hairdo I've ever seen. I mean now she IS rock, but I remember standing there and watching her and thinking she was either completely insane or that this was the weirdest thing I'd ever seen in my life! And the first time Throwing Muses ever toured with The Pixies everything was all camera. She was taking pictures of everything because everything was so exciting for her. She's still like that in a way. She really is a great person but there was a point in time when her old life overlapped with her new life and there was a very strange combination of people around her sometimes!

Eventually I wanted something of my own, outside The Breeders/ Muses/Pixies situation, because I had a huge backlog of songs that I wanted to use. I wanted to kind of set the tone with different people, with people who I felt were heading in the same direction I was, which I think Chris and Tom Gorman, at the time I found them, were. We had the same sensibilities. And it wasn't so much wanting to be a leader as it was just wanting something new and with people who hadn't yet influenced me. It would have been hard for me to do my songs with Kim Deal because she's been an influence in a lot of ways, so I don't think that it would have come out as true.

When Belly's first album, *Star*, came out, a lot of people were confused about my natural propensities towards bar chords and big choruses and big finishes and how it all juxtaposed with the imagery in the lyrics. I think it wasn't so much the imagery in itself that people found strange as the way it was pasted on top of the songs and the strange tension that created. It was particularly strange to me because I've always been attracted to that, my favourite songs are loaded with imagery and content, and I strive for that beauty and those layers. I like songs that you can listen to fifty times and still get something new out of.

I like fairy tales for that reason, and also because they're analogy-oriented and I'm the queen of analogy! I like folk tales. It probably links up with the anthropology I studied. I got really into symbolism and cultural relativity and how certain symbols have popped up in every culture since the beginning of time.

I think in some ways women get away with imagery a little more than men do. It goes along with women being put on pedestals. There's something more mysterious there, and there's more depth. It's the witchy thing. It's a questionable attitude, but it does give us more leeway in the psyche department!

I use female characters in my songs too, because obviously being female, I understand female situations a lot more. It's kind of sad in a way because it cuts off a whole half of the human race. I have tried to write from a male perspective, but it's always flat, it's too one dimensional for me. Female perspectives are limitless, but that is purely because I'm female.

Being in Belly was a little scary at first, especially as I was with all men in the beginning. It was really strange and it was very different. In the past I'd tended to go 'Oh it doesn't matter what the genders involved are', but it does to a certain extent, which is why when Fred Abong, my first bass player, left, I wanted a female because I wanted that balance.

Kristin always said that men play like rocks and women play like pebbles, and I'd always thought that was the case because we did play very intricately and we were always focussed on every other component of the band, and I did learn a lot from playing with her. But on the other hand Tom is a hundred times more sensual than I am. I don't want to say he plays like a woman, but he's very outwardly focussed, so once again a man comes into my life and throws some of my theories out of the window!

I think a lot of women guitar players are very melody-oriented as opposed to scale-oriented, and they tend to play outside of the usual parameters of what they're allowed to do, and Tom and I certainly do. But it is a very individual thing rather than a gender thing.

Having another woman on stage makes it less of a princessy situation though, you know like less of 'And here's the girl!' Before Gail Greenwood joined it was definitely like a 'Tanya and the boys' kind of thing. Unfortunately women are still treated like giraffes or something in music. It's still strange to see one on stage in 1994 which I think is ridiculous. I hope it's changing. It's definitely less of a big deal in America because there are more women in bands, or maybe it's just because there are a lot more bands!

It makes me feel more powerful to have another woman on stage and it makes me feel less precious, less special, less of a focal point. Tom and Chris become more important as individuals, it's a four-person thing, not three guys and a girl.

When Gail joined the reaction was such a toss-up. Half of the people were completely thrilled with her presence, and then there were people who said it threw off the mood and minimised the intensity. It made me really angry because nobody tells me who I play with, and I just don't think it's fair because people would say 'Oh she belongs in L7', and that's one of the most offensive things you could say about a woman because you're placing her in different types of categories—like she's not that type of woman. It was offensive to both of us.

If she were a man and she behaved the way that she does on stage she would just have been seen as eccentric. People seemed to see it out of context but she seems to be so completely in keeping with us that I didn't understand at first.

People must have thought I was fey by contrast or something as well. It's part of the way I carry myself, I'm not going to deny that, but people do tend to project some kind of fragility and preciousness on me that I find damages me. It's not something that I see but when I read it it always startles me and for a while I thought I had to do something about myself. Like I have to have a schtick, I don't have a schtick!

I think it has come to the point where people are more used to Gail and I being together, and also I think we have drifted more towards each other in some ways. I feel a lot more comfortable on stage so I move more, and she doesn't stick her bass up my ass in the middle of 'Low Red Moon' anymore!

But being put on a pedestal is the most degrading thing in the world and I don't think that a lot of male journalists understand that that kind of minimising adoration is really offensive to most women. They don't think about it. There was one guy, whose name I won't mention, who wrote a piece about me and kept going on about how cute and how tiny I was, that I was like a doll, and the whole thing was set up in this really dreamy way as if something beautiful was happening, and it just made me feel like nothing. It takes all of your power away for somebody to call you a doll. I don't think they're conscious of it though. Their appreciation takes on this thing like they're dealing with angels and not human beings.

It does happen to men too, though, pop idols and male actors especially. People like Brad Pitt and Johnny Depp—everything that I read about them is really insulting too. It's all about the phenomenon. Obviously, whether or not they're good, they're still doing something which is a job for them, something they're passionate about and it's minimising for them to be treated in that way.

It did damage my confidence a little. I take everything with a grain of salt for the most part but there are some things which really stick in my craw and the smallness thing is probably the biggest problem. When they go on about my tiny little hands and how everything about me is so sweet, I hate it.

I think the most ridiculous thing that's happened to me was the Riot Grrls attacking me for not being a 'real' woman though. By doing so, they were buying into the stories relayed by the very same male journalists they were claiming to undermine! They're anything but feminists to me if they're going to attack a woman in public for practising her art. It's really hypocritical and it's self-defeating to attack a woman in public if you're female unless it's for something extreme. I don't know how you can call yourself a feminist and spend all your time focussing on tearing down other women. It just doesn't make sense, it's a crazy platform and there's no foundation to it.

I understand their anger, obviously, I have the same anger, but they don't focus it on the right people. They scream and yell at 15-year-old boys to stand at the back of the room at rock concerts, and that's the wrong target. They're striking out at what's closest to them, what threatens them in their little clubs, not at what threatens them the most in the real world.

I'm not going to throw the baby out with the bathwater though. There are a lot of bands coming out of that movement with incredibly talented musicians and good songwriters who are very focused. They know exactly what they're doing, they educate themselves, and they know what they're talking about. But I have a hard time with people who picked up a guitar yesterday and then start attacking me. I mean, I know I'm not the most accomplished musician in the world but I have been playing for over ten fucking years and I have been working my ass off and I honestly don't think that I'm presenting an image that's going to harm the female struggle.

I think it's really sad that women are pitted against each other and it does happen and we do fall for it to a certain extent. Even in daily life you always come across a female who has this competitive thing and it just makes me want to slap them because it's just so obnoxious.

I thought that by now gender wouldn't be an issue for women in bands. When Throwing Muses first started it would come up and it always sounded like we were lying but it was really not something we thought about. It just never occurred to us that it would be any different to anything else, but I'm older and wiser now and I understand the difference and I understand the importance of it.

Although I do wish it weren't so much of an issue, I think talking about it is important and I do think that women still have a hard time feeling comfortable expressing themselves in a certain way. Most of us don't do it for a rock reason, a 'Look at me!' reason. There's not so much a sense of exhibitionism with women in bands, so in some ways maybe it's more of an uncomfortable position sometimes. But I don't think the issue is ever going to go away.

If the music world became glutted with all-women bands it would be a ridiculous issue, I mean it would become redundant. I think it's easing off a little bit because there are a lot more females involved now, and I think also if it gets to the point where there are more women playing guitar as opposed to being frontpeople, if the musicianship becomes as female-filled as the frontperson side of it, attitudes will change.

I think that if different types of women become well known—and I mean different bodies and attitudes and everything that goes along with the million types of women that there are—and I think if women could learn to be as unattractive as men are allowed to be, I think that would go a long way towards demystifying females in bands. That's why The Breeders are really positive because they're very natural, and you know Kim doesn't take a bath for a week at a time!

I remember a year ago doing an interview where I said why aren't women allowed to look like Kurt Cobain, or Michael Stipe—I mean they're both beautiful men obviously, but they're untidy. And Dave Pirner and Mark Lanegan and people like that. And basically Kim and Kelley and Josephine have done that. They're beautiful obviously, so in some ways it doesn't break the rules that much, but still, they don't do themselves up. They just put on whatever's closest to them when they get up!

I think the fact that Patti Smith was the first really frank woman was what made her so strong. She wasn't afraid of being ugly—and I don't mean physically—she allowed herself to be ugly, to sound ugly and to say ugly things and she did so in a very feminine way. There was nothing boyish about her, she didn't try to denounce her femininity, she was strong within the bounds of womanhood and she didn't put on any bravado. And it was the same with Chrissie Hynde. When I first saw her on the television I thought she was the coolest person in the world!

I don't feel ugly without make up on, it still has an element of dressing up to me, even at the ripe old age of 27, and it's fun for me But it does have this element of masking. It's not so much about prettifying as about changing and covering up almost. The moments when I've felt most beautiful have been when I've not had any make up on and I've been face to face with someone who loves me. That's when I feel pretty. Make up's always been something I'd save for somebody. It's a superficial, external example of the way that I act in general, the way that I give things up to people.

Sexuality is a huge part of your life and the person that you focus that energy on becomes a huge part of your life, whether that person is male or female. It's weird because I happen to be a committed heterosexual and that's pretty unfashionable now. I've experienced a backlash in this sense too, because I've talked about my boyfriends in interviews. And I thought the point of feminism was for women to make their own choices!

It comes back to my persona problem because the backlash made me sound like I was boy crazy or dependent, but love is a huge part of my life. Being able to give yourself to another person is the bravest thing in the world and it's the bravest thing I ever do. And if a guy in a band talks about his girlfriend, people think he must be a good person!

I've never altered the course of my life for a man, a man has never run my life, a man has never even taken care of the details of my life. I've always taken care of myself, I've almost been too much in the driver's seat sometimes, but on the other hand when I'm involved with somebody they affect my emotional life which has a lot to do with what I do, once I get past that point where I'm angry.

It's hard for me to talk about right now because I had a relationship where I was engaged and it didn't work out and a lot of things changed for me, as far as my ability to maintain something like that goes. But it's strange because I really honestly believe that you go through believing the stage you're in and that's important because if you do anything else, like if you say 'Well this happened to me last time so this time I'm going to be this way', you stop growing. I think it's really important to live in the moment too and I really do believe that if you get your ass kicked you get your ass kicked! And if you break somebody's heart, or somebody breaks your heart, that's the way it goes. Growth is the only important thing in the world and people get hurt unfortunately.

What I'd really like some day is a big huge family, definitely. I don't think I'd give up music for it so it's not something which will be possible for a while, I mean, I watched Kristin do it and she ended up being successful, but it was very difficult for her and I don't know if I have that kind of backbone. It's the kind of thing that you have to make provisions for and I know that when I have children they will be my focus and I want to be able to be in a position to deal with that, so I'm going to set up for it financially. And that's definitely a privilege.

But the other day I went to see Juliana Hatfield play in Boston and Dig was opening for them and I guess the lead singer's wife is about to have a baby and so they're only doing four shows at a time so he can fly home because she's just about to go and he wants to be there. And this guy, who is actually a friend of mine, was standing backstage saying how it was so cool that he should arrange the tour around her and what an exceptional husband he was, and later on that night I was having a conversation with somebody about wanting to have a child, and it wasn't even his goddamned conversation but he said, 'You can't have a baby now, you've got too much to do.' And I was like, 'Wait, do you know that you've said two things in one evening?' And this was a friend of mine, an intelligent man!

But it is unfair that if I got pregnant now it would mean renegotiating a contract. It makes me angry. It can be done though and of course it's hard but lots of things are hard,. Raising a child is hard anyway. Children are so strong, they're like little crazy people! At some point in my life I want a houseful of that kind of noise though!

Credentials

Band:	Belly
Signed to:	4AD in Britain, Sire in America
Managed by:	Gary Smith at Fort Apache
Past bands:	Throwing Muses
	The Breeders
Select discography:	See Kristin Hersh for Throwing Muses
	The Breeders—*Pod* LP (1990)
	Safari EP (1992)
	Belly—*Star* LP (1993)

Siobhan Fahey

'*They* don't expect boys to pretend to be nice, but
they do with girls, and I'm not a nice person, I'm a person!'

Siobhan Fahey

Introduction

Having trashed the grinning blonde of Bananarama dance routines and synchronised singing several years ago, Siobhan Fahey has re-emerged as a witty, subversive pop star with her own project, Shakespears Sister. With dramatic effect she questions the role of traditional beauty. Twisting the trappings of glamour into something dangerous, she mocks the perfection of cosmetic masks by smearing black eyes onto a faultless foundation, drawing scarlet dots on her cheeks and wearing deathly pale or deeply dark lips. Her carefully-crafted songs contain tales of badness, shattering the innocence and false nicety of the female pop persona, and her performances are deranged and out of control.

Now 36, Fahey was constantly moved around during the first years of her life because of her father's jobs. Her sense of security was deeply affected and she has since felt completely at odds with society as a whole. An oddball child who was forced to study, she was reared in a Victorian atmosphere as a Catholic, and is still seeking ways to express her sexuality.

Her one consolation was pop music, although she didn't find the confidence to pursue it as a career until years later when she moved to London and finally found herself in the girl gang she'd always longed for. Together with her friends Sarah Dallin and Keren Woodward, Fahey secured a record deal and Bananarama went on to become one of the most successful girl groups of all time. Eventually, though, she grew frustrated by the lack of song-writing possibilities and when the production team of Stock, Aitken and Waterman brought their homogenous sound to Bananarama, Fahey quit to discover herself anew.

Pop is stubbornly resistant to such transformations as Fahey's. Her previous existence with Bananarama was perceived to be lit-tle more than a 'masturbatory fantasy' by at least one sad male music critic and the fact that she wrote a hit song for the group about date rape, 'Robert de Niro's Waiting' is hardly common knowledge. Fahey willingly admits that her former pop career deteriorated into a game of manipulation and superficiality, but she also believes that Bananarama's original punk ethic was never fully appreciated.

Despite the derision Bananarama inspired, Fahey's leap into more serious realms, initially on her own, and later with the Los Angeles based singer/songwriter Marcella Detroit, was widely accepted and in February 1992, Shakespears Sister reached number one in the British charts with their single 'Stay'. She was never permitted to forget her 'embarrassing' past, but her new, more artistic role was celebrated immediately. Even her marriage to former Eurythmic Dave Stewart wasn't held responsible for her metamorphosis, much to her relief.

With Shakespears Sister, Fahey has used the frothy format of pop to make comments about the nastier side of female personal-ities. Her unhinged exterior lends weight to the sneering ironic humour of the songs, in which apologies are made and not meant, ill wishes are sent and bitchy mutterings are whispered beneath brilliant dance beats. The visual and lyrical trappings of pop are gleefully subverted with an almost hysterical power, freeing the

Women, Sex and Rock 'n' Roll

more frivolous end of entertainment from its vanilla trappings.

In addressing the darker side of female feeling, Fahey draws from her own self-doubt and confidence crises, empowering them through her songs by treating them positively and with humour, although her moodswings, depressions and emotional fevers fuel her artistic vision in a way that is neither romantic nor fantastical, but frighteningly real. Her battle to find a comfortable expression of sexuality has led her into caricaturing acceptable standards of female 'sexiness' and largely explains Shakespears Sister's popularity with women, most of whom are facing the same struggle daily.

By inscribing her negative feelings into the current pop charts, Fahey is confronting her pain, while opening up a Pandora's Box of suppressed female emotion for all the world to see. Glamour is often disturbed and Fahey is not only acknowledging that, she is celebrating it.

Siobhan Fahey

I don't have a hometown, I don't come from anywhere, I don't belong anywhere and that's always really freaked me out, to the point where my husband Dave's going, 'Why the fuck are we living in London?' and I just go, 'It's my home, I don't like it here but I live here! It's my home, I know people here!' I've been on this sort of neurotic search for a community to belong to for some time now. It's horrible, and it's probably the root cause of my alienation. I do feel very alienated from the rest of society and I have done forever really, so I don't know what I'd have done if I hadn't become a pop star really. It's the perfect job for people who don't fit in anywhere else.

When I was a child, my home life was pretty unstable. My dad just went where the work was basically. He was in the army for the first nine years of my life so I spent five years in Germany and then he was a contracting engineer so he'd just go wherever the money was. We lived all over Britain, in Scotland and all over England. It was horrible because I went to eight different schools, and you know what a nightmare it is starting a school. So by the time I went to my eighth one I was 14 and it was so traumatic I never really got over it. And I became completely—you know the girl in the class that everyone laughs at and no one sits next to? That was me. And I had to cope with that from 14 onwards.

I wasn't allowed to leave school, I had very strict parents, I wanted to leave at 16 and do my 'A' levels at a college but my parents wouldn't let me. It was an all-girls school and it was incredibly bitchy.

Actually, I did enjoy the convent I was at before that. It was like St Trinian's, it was very sweet. It was very strict but it was really antiquated and comforting and it had a community feel to it. But I left there and at the next one it was like 'Well, have you had sex yet?' I was 14 and I was really confused. So I mean I never got over that.

I was good at school as well, I got offered a place at Trinity in Dublin and at Edinburgh University as well, but I just wouldn't go because I resented so bitterly having been forced to stay at a school where I was really miserable, and I thought I was not going to university just because my parents wanted me to. I wanted to live and I wasn't living, I was existing, doing homework.

I completely identified with the punk thing because I felt that society rejected me at the age of 14, and I was considered a freak and an oddball, so I started to celebrate my oddness in the sixth year to survive. I used to dress in a really eccentric way and everybody thought I was a little bit nuts!

You can imagine my curiosity about what those girls from school are doing now. Every time I did *Top Of The Pops* I used to hope they were watching! And then there was this fantastic thing—I never, ever watch *Beadle's About*, but I saw a trailer for it once and it was about eight years ago, and there was this girl who used to be in my class, screaming her head off at Jeremy Beadle! She was this absolute cow of a girl who used to enjoy making me feel like a freak and she was being Beadled and it was fantastic because she hadn't changed at all. She was swearing her head off, and she lived in a really horrible house in Hatfield!

So that's why I became a pop star, to pay everyone back really!

I had no brothers and I went to all-girls schools and the only man I knew for years and years was my dad, so I suppose I do feel fairly uncomfortable with my sexuality. I get confused because I want to express it in a very pure way and it's very difficult to in our business, and that's a major reason why I do what I do. I can't express my sexuality socially because I'm very repressed in that way, so it's my way of celebrating it I suppose. But it's so monstrously overstated on stage that I always turn it into a joke because I'm so fucked up about it, if I see a woman flirting, I feel sick. So I sort of mock the whole thing— men's preconceptions of what a sexy woman's supposed to be like and look like and act like and it's like 'Fuck you!' It's a very easy thing to do! The Virgin/Whore thing is still very powerful.

Men may well be confused about it all too, but they handed us the mandate. It's a man's world and it's run on men's principles and the whole foundation of society is based on male guidelines. The natural order of events is that man impregnates a woman and she's the parent of the child, so the community should really be women and children, and the men go off and they're kind of floating things. So the hub of the community should naturally be women and kids. But then men wanted ownership over their children, so the natural set up of society, which should be these communes of women and children, was suddenly separated off and we're put into these little units and that's the basis of the society we live in now.

And so now we've got this massive confusion because of course we're sexual creatures and we're taught to feel dirty about it and we're still looking for a way to express it. We're all conditioned to enjoy looking glamorous and to appreciate that look, and it makes us feel good about ourselves to dress up, but even so, women do dress up for women, I really do believe that. We dress up for each other and not for men even though men think otherwise and will not believe that we don't dress up for them. And I think that's why people liked Shakespears Sister, because we dressed up for ourselves and then just completely took the piss out of the whole glamour thing anyway.

Dave's always saying that my problems with my sexuality are due to my Catholicism. Now I just don't believe it. I wasn't brought up any other way so I don't know for sure, I just think that there's more to it.

I did have this tenacious need to cling onto my Catholicism though. Not that I'd been a practising Catholic since I was 14, when I'd gone through this phase where I was bored at church and I thought it was terrible because my mind was wandering, and that I shouldn't go unless I was concentrating.

When I was about 13, I went through this really hysterical religious phase which apparently happens quite often in puberty. And I remember having a whole religious lesson devoted to vocations. I was told I'd make a great nun–'Margery Lemmon and Siobhan Fahey stand up! Yes girls, you have been called to serve the Lord, to marry Christ!' Even before the nun who was taking the lesson said it, I knew she was going to and I was thinking, no no! I didn't want to be a nun, religious as I was.

I ended up being massively hamstrung by my guilt about not wanting to be a nun. And it got to the point where, when I was about 14, I actually thought that the devil was trying to possess me. I mean seriously, I thought that. I couldn't go to sleep at night without being on my knees with my arms crossed. I was completely isolated apart from my sisters, but what could they do? They thought I had a screw loose, and they were used to that.

I still have a really freaky thing about what I do and I'm probably really fucked up about my sexuality partly because of that, because I was completely appalled with myself for not wanting to be a nun, but I was also determined that I wasn't going to be one. The teacher said if you have a religious vocation and you do not answer it, you will never be happy, you will never be at peace. And I've never found peace. And I still think that there's a fucked up side of me that still thinks, Jesus Christ! It's because of that!

I mean, I took six months off last year after touring with Shakespears Sister, because I really needed to be a mother to my kids. They were starting to suffer from my absence and I felt so guilty and wretched about that. When the six months was up I wanted to get back to writing again, but after a week, out of the blue, I ruptured a disc. And I've always had incredibly good health, I've never had anything like this happen to me, and it was like 'On your back woman, you're not doing anything.' It was like the universe was trying to tell me something—'You're not going to make another record.' And for three months I was on my back and I went through loads of therapy as well, because I got really fucked up. Anyway, slowly but surely I started writing again, and then I went on holiday to Jamaica for Christmas and when I came back I spent two days in the studio before I had a car accident. So I went to see this woman, who is so amazing, for therapy. I feel very ambivalent about therapy, I'm not sure that it actually can help, but I don't think it can do me any harm because I'm with this really fantastic woman. I just don't have tremendous faith in my ability to find peace.

But I did think, Jesus Christ, someone's trying to tell me I'm definitely not going to make a record. And I know why, it's because I'm an egomaniac, that's the only reason I make records, I should have been a nun! Well, not a nun, but I should be a mother, what the hell am I doing? I'm an egomaniac, the universe is punishing me! That's how much of a fucked-up Catholic I am. And I said this to

Women, Sex and Rock 'n' Roll

my therapist, and she told me no, and that I had the accidents to bring me to therapy. And she's not a normal therapist this woman, she's a healer. She healed my back without an operation which was incredible. The medical profession were going to operate on me and I was reading this book about how male doctors rip women open and pull kids out of women with forceps, and here were these male doctors telling me that I've got to have an operation, and I said, 'No way!' And this woman came in to see me and made me better. She's so fantastic, I don't like to take up her time, because I feel that I don't deserve it because I'm not suicidal. But she doesn't think that way, it's just me again!

I don't want to die feeling like this but it is the rub which keeps you going. You don't find happy people in bands, and I'm not talking about bass players and drummers, I'm talking about people who front bands, it's such a fucking weird thing to do. It's terrible though because none of us has it sussed. I can't stand songwriters who preach, because people who write songs are troubled people and they haven't got the answers. They can ask the questions eloquently or highlight things. I talk about my problems with myself a lot of the time in my songs. It is more about communication. Other people feel like that too and that's completely why I worship Morrissey's words, because he doesn't provide answers. And Joni Mitchell, she's fantastic. I got her album *Blue* when I was going through my religious mania phase, because that's when it came out, and it's one of my favourite albums of all time. It's an incredible record, she's a total genius.

I think every child is obsessed with pop music, and I was and it never went away. It was the only thing I ever really wanted to do, apart from when I was very young when I wanted to be an actress. I'd love to do some theatre now actually. But the pop thing never went away.

When I was young I started to learn the guitar and then we moved and everything changed and I was locked into this solitary world and I just had records. I couldn't even afford to buy records actually, except once in a blue moon, so I had the radio and I was a complete pop fanatic. I never used to miss the charts, and all the way though the 1970s I was a walking pop expert.

Dave and I always argue about the 1960s and the 1970s. He says all the amazing bands came out of the 1960s and made the 1970s look like a joke, but what was fantastic about the 1970s, I think, was the wit and humour and irony, the playful decadence and caricature I loved Bowie and Roxy Music all the way through the 1970s. But I never admitted it, I never admitted that I had a crush on Marc Bolan because of the Catholic weirdness in me. And that's odd, because when you're 12 or 13 you usually tell your best friend when you have a crush on a boy. But I would never admit to any sort of sexual feelings at all.

My sisters weren't the same. My sister who's closest to me in age started going out before me and she's a year younger. I didn't go out until I was 16 at least. I didn't have anyone to go out with. But she started going to discos and she shaved her eyebrows off and wore white tights and platform shoes and all that kind of thing. And I was such a freak, I had plaits, knee socks and flat shoes and one eyebrow across my forehead. I thought she looked like a tart, because I was so fucked up. And I'm still working at it! That's probably why at my age I'm still able to make records that count because I'm still totally disturbed from that time, which is the age of most record buyers. I'm not very mature for my age I suppose. My friend, the video maker Sophie Muller, says that I'm a 14-year old trapped in the body of a 35-year old!

Women, Sex and Rock 'n' Roll

During my adolescence I obviously felt really threatened by other girls and I couldn't express my sexuality in the way I dressed or anything. I used to have desperate crushes, which were like physical longings and they were really torturous actually. So maybe people should just have a shag and just get it out the way early on!

I first had sex around the time of my 18th birthday so I had to go through years of all this AAGGH! I was in love, it was a proper relationship and I had absolutely no guilt about it whatsoever and I enjoyed every minute of it and I have done ever since. Thank God all this stuff hasn't interfered with my ability to enjoy sex. But on the other hand I think it's boring if it goes on for too long. I can't believe that people can spend three hours having sex you know. And I see it very much as an animal thing, an animal act, it's part of nature and it's very pure in that way. If I'm hungry I eat, I don't like spending hours at a dinner table lingering over different kinds of food, and I'm like that about sex as well. If I want sex I want it there and then, and I don't like spending too long over it, but that might be to do with Catholicism again. I don't know, I don't really think it is.

I used to find solace in food during my adolescence as well, so my weight shot up. I was heavier at the age of 12 and 13 than I've ever been. I hated it so I started starving myself. I did it for a year and it was so annoying because I didn't really get very thin. I only lost half a stone, and because I was so depressed as well, my system ground to a halt. When I moved to London it was fantastic. I was out every night all night and I lived off beer and coffee and cigarettes because I couldn't afford to eat, and that sorted my body shape out immediately.

The thing is, anorexia is apparently directly related to your feelings about your own sexuality, and the repression of your own burgeoning womanhood basically, so that probably had more to do with my eating habits than anything.

I moved to London after refusing to go to Trinity College in Dublin. I was having a nervous breakdown at that point because my boyfriend had dumped me. It didn't go down too well with me because finally I'd found true love and of course we were going to get married, and then after a year and a half he dumped me. I didn't handle it very well, I was a raving lunatic for a good year! But my father was so devastated at my refusing to go to Trinity, he couldn't speak to me for years afterwards. He'd had a place there himself, but in those days Catholics needed the local Bishops' permission to go, because it was a Protestant college, and he'd been refused, so he'd ended up at University College in Dublin instead, getting pissed every day. It had been his dream for me to go, but I ended up going to London and getting pissed all the time as well!

I actually told my parents that I'd just take a year off before college. So they made me get a job. I started working at a Midland Bank in the city and I nearly went off my head. It was so horrific and so vile. I mean how can anybody agree to spend the next 25 years of their life where they're not allowed to wear what they want to, where there is no personal expression? I packed it in and went on the dole until I went to Decca record label where I worked as a receptionist for a year and a half. That was really boring too and they had nobody interesting on the label at all, but those were good times because I went out to see bands all the time.

Eventually I went back to college to do fashion journalism because I wanted to do something which involved writing. I never had the confidence to take control. You know how Toni Halliday says 'I'm in charge of my life and this is what I want to do so I'm doing this!'? Well, I wasn't like that at all. All I wanted to do was be in a band but I wouldn't dream of even telling anyone, in the same way that I wouldn't tell anyone if I had a crush. I would never go to an audition or place an ad or answer an ad or do anything like that. So I went and did journalism and that's when I met Sarah and Keren and they were similar to me because they were going to see bands every night and they were punks. We stood out like sore thumbs and they had much more in common with me than anyone else in that class: it was weird. This was a fashion journalism course and everyone was dressed in A-line skirts and button-up blouses. They looked like the same people who worked in the Midland Bank! I couldn't believe it. And the teachers were scared of me and Sarah, because we looked frightening to them. And it has to be said, we were quite snobby, we used to sit at the back and snigger at everyone. But at last I was part of the school gang, and that's what Bananarama was all about for me, it was fantastic.

It's a real shame because we started off as a really interesting band. It was like 'Well, fuck you, you want us to be pop stars? OK we'll be pop stars, it'll be a laugh, and yeah we can make records, we don't need to learn instruments. Give us a contract!' And it was so easy, we didn't have to do anything! But of course everything became homogenised, we became toothy girls. Our original attitude was brilliant, but we hadn't paid our dues. We didn't think we had to, and I don't regret anything that happened, but I didn't learn to write songs until I was already a pop star.

I was escaping the fucked-up Catholic thing. I'd found my girl gang and I was having a laugh and I was just chasing a good time because I hadn't had a good time up until then and I never wanted the party to stop. So the band probably suffered from a degree of superficiality! But we didn't develop into anything. We should have developed then into Shakespears Sister. What Shakespears Sister is, is the way I always imagined Bananarama would be, but I was one of three people, so I couldn't present them with personal lyrics, I could never express myself as a songwriter in the way I wanted to.

Our song 'Robert de Niro's Waiting' was actually about date rape The girl in the song was raped so she didn't trust anybody afterwards 'Boys living next door are never what they seem' is what that line's about. This boy's raped her and she's completely paranoid and she thinks everybody's out to get her so she escapes into a world of fantasy and she trips out in her head. But you'd never know it. Nobody gets it! And I tried to say in an interview once that it was about rape, but Sarah and Keren just wouldn't have it. That's what I had to cope with—'Don't you get above your station, young lady!' I guess they obviously felt threatened but I didn't know how to handle it and I had to do most of the work, I was the driving force. They were very lazy, they just used to watch Martin Scorsese films all day and things like that!

Instead of being able to develop as a songwriter I just had to work with people I didn't like. I didn't like Pete Waterman at all. I couldn't be in the studio with him. We really fell out very early on because his attitude was appalling. I mean he's good for a laugh—to laugh at. Everything he says is such a gem and you just cannot believe this moron and the stuff he comes out with. So for sheer entertainment value he was top notch! But he's got a good punter's ear and that's what he boasts about, his punter's ear, but I'm far too passionate about music to write songs that are hit clichés. My whole thing is trying to make hit records that have some sort of originality or meaning, or preferably both.

Pop music has got a really bad name and with Shakespears Sister I think I reminded people that it is possible to make pop music of value and worth but I owed that to the public because of what I allowed Bananarama to turn into. I was partly responsible for that. I wanted to leave about a year before I did, but if I had done I'd have been homeless, jobless, penniless and friendless. Being in a band involves a very strange interdependence which makes people feel very insecure and neurotic, and you should never believe that any band ever splits up in any way except acrimoniously, because it's more intense than a marriage, apart from the fact that you don't usually have sex with the other band members. With Bananarama, all our friends were mutual so the whole fabric of my situation was bound up with theirs.

I tried to leave before we made that last album but they talked me into staying and I'm glad I did because it was a hugely successful record. The thing that really annoyed me was that people would always write us off every time we made a record, but we'd be back on top of the charts, just when they thought it was safe! It was sheer bloody-mindedness a lot of it! It was a good time to leave after that.

Meeting Dave did help actually. The Eurythmics must have started about the same time as we did, and I must have met him in a studio or something. I don't remember the very first meeting, but I do remember when he first asked me out. He rung up and asked me to the pictures and I was going out with someone else at the time but I really liked Dave, I really wanted to get to know him. I felt really, really comfortable with him which is completely unheard of for me, to feel comfortable with someone I'd only just met, but I felt like I already knew him, it was so weird. I really wanted to be his friend at least, even though I had a boyfriend. But I told him I couldn't go to the pictures. So then he rang up and said, 'Well, do you want to come and see my recording studio, The Church?' and I said I couldn't because Sarah and Keren would think it was strange if I went out without them. So he said, 'Well OK, you can bring them'. So we all went! And then we bumped into him really infrequently over the years because they were always on tour and it was really weird because I went to see a psychic in Tokyo in 1984, and the psychic told me I'd already met the person I was going to marry, and that he was a bit older than me, and it wasn't the boyfriend I was with at the time. She told me to get rid of my present boyfriend because he was terrible! This psychic in the street told me that, and it was so weird. I didn't want to hear it at the time because I liked my boyfriend but it all turned out to be very true.

I completely expected everybody to say Dave was my Svengali figure, and I can't believe I got away with it, to tell you the truth. I really did expect it though, because there I was in Bananarama, and then I came out with Shakespears Sister. I was incredibly relieved that it didn't happen.

In fact Dave had more to do with *Sacred Heart*, the first record, than I've ever admitted to. I wouldn't admit to it because he hadn't made me, they were my songs that I'd written and I had produced the record with my friend Richard Feldman who was a neighbour across the road from us in Los Angeles, but Dave co-wrote some of the songs and he was around when we were mixing. Not that he mixed it for us, but at one point we'd been in the studio for eight hours and it still sounded monstrous, and he walked in and said something like 'Oh just put a repeat on this' and we took his advice and the mix went back on course. He could do something to it which just made it sparkle.

He's a great producer and he was very helpful. But he didn't make my record, I made my record. I mean I'm married to him, he was around and if he'd popped in for five minutes, well, five minutes with Dave is worth a day with someone else and that's the truth. The ideas are just tripping off his tongue. They're all good ideas, but they're not all appropriate. He said that someone recently said he was like

Willy Wonka, and he was pissing himself laughing, but he makes everybody believe in themselves. He recognises the worth in everybody around him, and instils them with the confidence to be who they really are, which is why he's got the world queuing up. That's why all those people like Mick Jagger call him up, because he's such an inspiring person and a lovely person and a very, very special person. I'm very lucky to be married to him, I don't think he's lucky to be married to me! I don't know how he copes, I don't know how he puts up with me. It's no picnic!

I made the transition to Shakespears Sister very tentatively and nervously. Basically, it started with this idea I had of an ever-changing, shifting conglomerate of people that I'd put around me. I saw it as my solo thing. I started writing with Richard Feldman, and he suggested Marcy, an old girlfriend of his, could do backing vocals. So that's how I started working with her.

I altered my looks and dyed my hair black to get away from the blonde thing and because it makes me feel much more powerful. White platinum blondes can often be as powerful because it's such an extreme look and it's making a mockery of the whole blonde thing, but unfortunately as I'd found out with Bananarama, if you make a mockery of it, people don't get the joke. With Shakespears Sister things have always been a bit more unhinged. It's like we had this perfect glamorous exterior but we're really losing it. Unhinged and proud of it!

The thing about Bananarama was that we were all supposed to be really nice people and not at all bitchy. But women are labelled as bitches if we're in any way assertive and so we go around pretending we're these vapid creatures who don't have a dark side. Every single month I'm a total bitch for at least a week of it. And nature's designed it so that women never get complacent with our lives, and we don't because every month we go, 'Oh, everything's fucking awful!' And I behave badly and I think horrible things and that's part of my experience. Nobody has ever admitted to being a bad person in a song, but with Shakespears Sister I have. '16th Apology' from our second album, *Hormonally Yours*, is full of irony, because I'm apologising for being bad, but not really! The first single, 'Break My Heart' was a really bitchy lyric too, and although I was nervous at the video shoot because I'd never performed alone before, and I didn't know if I could carry it, it was natural to me.

I'm still trying to come to terms with that side of myself because I hate myself, I really do. I really have got massive problems with myself. I was brought up in a very Victorian way where girls were seen and not heard, and should be submissive and docile and pleasant. And I'm none of those things so I go through this thing where I think what a horrible person I am. And I'm actually not a horrible person at all, but I torture myself with the more hideous aspects of myself, and I even do it in songs! I sort of laugh about it in a way because I go to therapy but do I really want to change? Can I change? You can't really change, can you?

The time when I feel empowered is when I'm performing because I can really inhabit that side of myself with complete aplomb and really enjoy being that thing. I don't even see it as an alter ego, I see it as very much the real me. I see it as the place where I can enjoy being who I really am.

With Shakespears Sister I used to feel really invincible and I used to walk off stage at the end of every gig covered in bruises. I've chipped a tooth, blacked my eye, and once I tripped over Marcy's guitar lead, smashed into the backline and knocked everything over completely! I was in another world and I was completely unfettered and I loved it. And I could go 'Well, fuck off if you don't like me, but you do like me, don't you?' And in real life I'm not like that, I'm really repressed. It's such a fucking cliché, but I really am at home on the stage and that's why I wish I'd started a proper band ten years ago, because I could have spent more time gigging, I would've loved it. Unfortunately I left it until I was the mother of two children. But at least I've had the experience and I've enjoyed it and I'll find other avenues for performance.

So working with Marcy was good for a while, but basically it was a recipe for disaster and I should've learned my lesson by then, but you see I like working with other people. Although I wanted to be the creative controller, I didn't like the idea of being a solo artist because it seemed uninteresting and I was afraid of being alone. I hate being on my own because I'm terrified of what's in my head and that's why I co-write, because I can't be in a room on my own.

By the time it came to the second album Marcy wanted more of a profile. I didn't want to be unfair to her, she was singing and co-writing so I thought she ought to be in Shakespears Sister with me. She wanted fifty per cent of everything, so I said OK, as long as I remained in the driving seat. And we actually worked really well together, but it was weird because socially we didn't gel at all. As people we just did not click.

The problem was I always had this big ethos about bands growing up together and it irks me to see something put together. It's outrageous that people thought Bananarama were put together! So even though we worked well together it felt strange because we weren't friends. But then I thought, well look at the trouble I got in last time I worked with friends, maybe this will be better. But it wasn't really because although Marcy's got an amazing voice, I don't particularly like good voices actually. Her voice worked well with mine, because I have a pop sensibility and to make good pop records it really helps to have a good backing vocalist, but when it started becoming more than that, I just thought, OK, the next record will just be me. It'll still be Shakespears Sister, because Shakespears Sister is me. You live and learn!

I'd like to make a record which pays no heed to the pop charts, although pop is my great love, but then I love The Breeders and I think they're pop music. I really don't see the divide between indie and pop, I think it's such a shame that it's all split into different categories. I'm torn between being a rock hag from hell which I really would love and something that's more introverted where the words play a bigger role. And I love disco records but I also love Joni Mitchell and I also love Patti Smith so I'll probably be writing things which are reminiscent of all those things. Maybe I should just sling 'em all on the same record! Do you remember Mike Yarwood used to say 'And this is me' at the end of his TV programme? Well I've always wanted to call my solo album that, but nobody would get the joke!

I don't see the two things I've done as so incredibly different; I see the thread and the thread is me. I think that there was a lot of humour and irony to what Bananarama did but I think probably we didn't express it properly. Sophie Muller and I share the same sense of humour and she didn't get the joke and it's disappointing, but then we weren't working with the right people. I used to perceive what I was doing in that band through my eyes and so I didn't see the crassness of it because I knew the intent. When people said we were blonde bimbos I couldn't believe it!

But you know I still see it now. I don't read women's magazines but I opened one the other day and there was a thing about girl groups in it. The quotes could have been Bananarama quotes from 12 years ago, but the photographs! The tragedy with us women is that we have all this intent but we're so brainwashed by society and these magazines that we don't realise. We put on our red lipstick like we do every day, we highlight our hair, we wear fashionable clothes because that's what all women do—very few don't—because that's what girls do, society tells us this is what we do. And those girls just didn't look powerful in the photographs.

I felt sorry for those girls and it did make me wonder how far we've come in the last 12 years. OK, they're playing their instruments, but before Bananarama there were The Slits and they were amazing, they were completely in control. I'm sure those girls are in control too, but they don't realise how society can fuck up what you do and say, and that they were being fucked up there and then by that photographer.

There was a really nice quote from this group Voodoo Queens but it didn't come across in the photos. And I've been there! It made me feel better about myself because I'm always beating myself up that I didn't take more artistic control. We never did sexual poses or anything like that, but they wouldn't make a boy band stand close together with their arms round each other. And you do it because it would be churlish not to do it. They don't expect the boys to pretend to be nice, but they do with girls, and I'm not a nice person, I'm a person!

Credentials

Band:	Shakespears Sister
Signed to:	London Records
Managed by:	Eligible Management
Past bands:	Bananarama
Select discography:	*Sacred Heart* LP (1989)
	Hormonally Yours LP (1992)

Marianne Faithfull

'*I'm* afraid to say that I think we have a problem with the humanity of women and that this is not recognised ... You're either allowed to be sappy and romantic ... or angry and vicious, but you're not allowed to express the other things.'

Marianne Faithfull

During the 1960s Marianne Faithfull was the girl every woman wanted to be and the girlfriend every man wanted. Known mainly for her controversial career as a Rolling Stone consort, she had already spent two years as a pop singer before she became entangled in a life with Mick Jagger, although her independence was quickly consumed by the brilliant circus surrounding her lover. Her confidence was brutally bitten into, and while she revelled in Jagger's reflected glory for a while, the need for her own, coupled with her damaged self-esteem, drove her to sacrifice her ultimately shadow-like existence for a place on the street as a heroin addict.

A decade of drugs later, Marianne Faithfull was back riding on the wave of punk's energy with *Broken English*, a startling collection of songs nursing all manner of unbridled female emotion, from irrational guilt to crudely honest sexual jealousy. The record received shocked, outraged and even scathing reviews, but in the main it was critically acclaimed and has since become a classic. Finally, Faithfull had earned the respect she'd longed for, as an artist in her own right, after nearly killing herself to get it.

Descended from a line of Austrian aristocracy, Marianne Faithfull's mother, Eva, was of the Sacher Masoch family, sharing the blood of Leopold Sacher Masoch, who in 1870 wrote the most infamous of his sexual novels, *Venus In Furs*, giving rise to the term 'masochism'. Born at the very end of 1946, Faithfull was educated at St Joseph's Convent School in Reading after her parents had separated. She was never attracted by pop music as a young teenager, although she did entertain ideas of becoming an artist, and when she met The Rolling Stones' manager, Andrew Oldham, at a launch party for his new act, Adrienne Posta, in 1964, the chance was offered to her.

Oldham knew instantly that he could sell Faithfull to the public with her beauty and a quaint song written by Keith Richards and Mick Jagger, 'As Tears Go By'. And while her early recordings never provided her with more than moderate success, she quickly become a 1960s icon.

Married at 18 to her boyfriend of roughly three years, Indica art gallery owner and avant garde intellectual, John Dunbar, Faithfull was also a mother by 1965, juggling like hell to keep her career together, and she grew bored and tired with domesticity within just over a year. The charms of Mick Jagger, whom she'd met through Oldham, proved irresistible and in 1966 she embarked on a four-year relationship with the rising star which was to stain her life. In the face of the almighty Rolling Stones, Faithfull felt compelled to surrender her own comparatively ineffective pop career, and even her attempts at acting were finally upstaged by Jagger who decided to follow her into film.

Until she made *Broken English* in 1979, Faithfull was identified as a has-been girlfriend, famous for doing nothing, and while she now enjoys respect and artistic recognition, her own decision to opt out of second-hand fame has always been perceived as an unforgivable weakness, especially as her alternative to Jagger's court was heroin. Stereotyped as a fallen angel, she has been forced to live with the legacy of her former innocence and glamour, both of which owe more to exaggerated folk myths than the truth of a real woman's experience. Her descent into addiction has been morbidly gloated over, unlike the self-destructive habits of her male contemporaries which have often been perceived almost romantically, and her return to rock has labelled her a survivor first and foremost, when, as she points out, she is so much more than that.

Having written her autobiography, *Faithfull*, acted in two new movies, *Shopping* and *When Pigs Fly*, and completed a new album with Angelo Badalamente (famed for his *Twin Peaks* soundtracks) Faithfull now appears to be more satisfied with her life than ever. Yet in terms of women's history in rock culture, her own perspectives on the more turbulent periods of her life during the 1960s and 1970s are deeply interesting and throw a clear light over an experience which has often been confusedly portrayed. Marianne Faithfull deserves to be known for far more than her teenage image, her ex-lover, her attempted suicides and her battlewounds, but until these are each demystified they will continue to haunt her.

Marianne Faithfull

In Her Own Words

I grew up in Reading and was educated at St Joseph's Convent, although I really got my education through reading. I remember my mother saying to me—and this was in direct contrast to what the nuns were saying to me at the convent—that I could read anything I liked and there was nothing I couldn't read, and she completely trusted me. And I did, I read anything I liked.

Of course at school there was the Roman Catholic index of books which Catholics are not supposed to read. It's amazing, it goes from things like Stendhal and Fielding, and even certain Shakespeare works right down to *The Bedroom Philosophers* and that sort of thing. And I actually started to go through it with my best friend, Sally Oldfield, whose brother was Mike Oldfield. We read every book on it, systematically, including de Sade! I don't know what it did for us really, I think it was kind of daft but it definitely broadened our outlook, and it was frightfully good for the vocabulary!

I didn't actually like *The Bedroom Philosophers*. I liked the concept but I didn't like the book, but on the other hand it's very interesting stuff especially when you write songs and it's always been there in me. In fact one of the things I realised in writing my own autobiography was how masochistic I am in my own life. Not directly as in wanting to be whipped until I die, but just from the emotional point of view, and I've used it in my songs. I don't quite understand

144

it actually, I've got to read the book again, although I don't really want to!

When I was a child, I think my mother kept a lot of her life from me. I'm sure that's one of the reasons I went to boarding school, because she wanted to have a life for herself. I found out later that she was having affairs. I think I even knew at the time, yeah, I did because she used to tell me but I didn't really think about it. I just remember being 12, 13, 14 and looking at my mother with wonder and amazement and thinking if only I could just be grown up and drink and smoke! I thought it would all be fabulous! But not sex. I didn't think about the sex at all, or how she and her lovers managed it.

She wasn't a person of complicated words, but she was incredibly graceful and she taught me about dance and movement, but I wish she'd shown me more. I look back and I have no memory of Eva with a man. I have no memory of her at all like that. I do not know how she related in a relationship, if she was in love or in hate. I mean I know how she acted with my father, but I was very young then and that was my only impression. I haven't got the information about how she was with people she had affairs with and I now regret that very much because I feel there's a whole thing I don't know and for years I've been trying to hammer it out for myself. I feel like there's a big piece missing and I don't trust myself at all. If I'd seen Eva doing it it might be different, but she never allowed that. I suppose we must have been made very differently because I don't think she really got that involved with people. I don't think she was a romantic person in any way and I don't think she was emotional. I think she just took it as her due and her right. Although she did like very clever men and I do too, that's what really turns me on about people.

I was really waiting for someone to come along and turn me into an artist. I really wanted it desperately for years. I don't know where they are now and when Eva died I couldn't bear to sort everything out and I didn't, my son Nicholas did it, but my mother kept the rough books I had at school. I hadn't got it yet that my name was *the* name, I thought I had to change my name, so I would make names up instead of Marianne Faithfull in these rough books, so obviously I was dying for someone to come along and find me.

It's incredible now that I and Eva just said 'Sure' to Andrew Oldham though, and I've been through times in my life when I've been furious with her for doing that, because I was a minor and she signed my contract. It depends how you see it and I don't mean this literally, you must try and see how I mean it, but there have been times when I've felt like I was just sold. And I think Eva regretted it, because I think she felt that if she'd held on longer she would have got more for me, but I wanted it. I remember in the last five years of her life we did talk about these things. Our relationship got very good and we loved each other terribly, and we discussed all these things, and she said to me, and I have to believe her, and I do believe her, that at the time I was so determined that there was nothing she could do to stop me, so she thought she might as well let me do it.

I wasn't terribly into pop music, but I didn't care! That's the fascinating thing and I'm still like that, and I've never understood why people can't accept the fact that I didn't dream of being a pop singer! There is an area of regret, I know if I'd worked harder and trained more, I could have done a lot of things. I had a beautiful voice and I could have become a great Brechtian interpretive singer and I could have probably been a very much better actress. But actually I do think I did the right thing, because pop was what was happening at the time, and I could sense that. I knew when I met Andrew that he actually had his finger on it.

I loathed the way my pop career developed though. I've never been wild about going on tour, I get tremendous stage fright and I always have and I always will, but I always saw that it was very important and what I do like is the charge of the audience. And that has its disadvantages of course and they are serious disadvantages after all, but I do like connection, and of course in those days I wasn't very good at it yet but it still happened a lot and I still remember astounding moments that made up for all of it.

I guess what I didn't like was the sleaze, the cheap way it was seen because I had tremendous artistic snobbery. I felt like they did it very cheaply, and it was true. It was just before the great leap of Andy Warhol and pop art, when everything like that really became art, and I did not see myself like Lulu or Helen Shapiro at all, and I did not like being put into that bracket, but then again I wasn't always. There were real moments when people obviously could see what I was about. Andrew could, and I remember on my first tour, there was a great promoter in England, Tito Burns, who worked together with an agent on these tours who could see something in me too.

I was 17 and I'd never been on the stage before and we were at the Hammersmith Palais I think, and we were rehearsing and I did my little thing which was very peculiar really. It was basically doing 'As Tears Go By', 'Greensleeves' and a couple of others, it was so daft! But Tito Burns was there in the auditorium and he must have seen something coming out, something I can't see, because it's like trying to look into your own eyes or kiss your own lips, it's impossible. But obviously something happened and he saw that and I'll never forget it, it was the first time I got some real feedback. I'd done eight minutes and he said, 'Right, make it 15.' It was amazing because there were 16 acts and we all had a set time, and I got 15 minutes which was extraordinary and I knew that. I was very bright and I could see immediately I'd made a big impression.

At the time I didn't know or care about being seen as an icon of the times, or having lots of other girls wanting to be me so there's no point in getting sentimental about it now! I did have heartstopping moments when I was working on my autobiography and I saw all the old pictures of myself though. A lot of them were from agencies and a lot of them were useless, but there was one which was obviously from the first tour and it was obviously taken on the roof of the Gaumont or somewhere and I look amazingly bored. You can see my eyes glazing over with boredom at these local newspaper people. But it's an amazing picture of this lovely child with all this hair and everything, so now I can see it, but I really didn't then.

I remember typical adolescent stuff. I remember only wanting to be thinner like Sandie Shaw, and I wanted to sound like Dusty Springfield and look like Goldie and The Gingerbreads. You always want what you don't have at that age, although I suppose I'd have done something about it if I really had wanted to.

I used to see all these girls on *Ready Steady Go* and I felt very bogged down because I never felt like them. They did a lot of sheer pointless jigging about which I thought was dreadful and which was completely against my whole sort of learned attitude about everything. I had a real stillness about me and I think I got it from the nuns at the convent. That's how they were. They didn't walk, they glided, and their faces didn't move. They kept what I suppose you'd call a modest demeanour. I wasn't trying to be modest or saintly in any way, although that was something which came through. I was just very, very nervous.

The first television thing I did was for *Juke Box Jury* and they talked about you and played your record and you were behind a screen. And I watched it the following week at Sally's house, and to my horror I could see that I was so nervous that my knees were knocking. I could actually see that I was shaking. And I must have thought to myself that whatever happens I must never ever show that kind of fear again. So I must have made myself absolutely still and it was really from pure terror.

Of course it's the best way to do it for the material that I did, and now I understand much more about it having done *The Threepenny Opera* at Dublin's Gate Theatre in 1991 and having worked with the playwright Frank Guinness and read all that stuff about Brecht and of course it's an extraordinary thing. It is. It's almost alienation. And it's 'No, you may not be part of mine, you may not be me'. It's real arrogance even if it does come out of fear and it was very powerful, especially from someone so young. To put your nose in the air and stand completely still and stare with a steely blue gaze has an effect.

I didn't actually feel superior to other people at all though. The thing I loved about touring was that it really opened me up to some of those people, like The Hollies, and they were great. It was pretty extraordinary being 17 and earning all that money and holding my own on a tourbus with 30 guys! I had a chaperone who was my friend and we had these great tour romances. We had great fun, and it really worked, and I hate to think what would have happened if I'd stayed at the convent and gone to Cambridge or Oxford or RADA. Well RADA would have been all right, but it was great meeting all those guys in the bands. They were very sweet to me, and now I can see how amazing I must have been for them. They were pretty scared of me actually, but they were very kind.

Of course 1964 in rock'n'roll wasn't at all a liberating time for women. But Tony Calder and Andrew who were my managers at the time, never, never told me what to do. They never told me what to wear or how to move. They just sent me out there and I was on my own and it was amazing. I was very lucky because if I'd have got one of those people who tried to change you I wouldn't have been able to do it. But the fact that they liked my attitude and what I did, and trusted it, was extraordinary, and nobody has ever quite got that. They all think that everybody in the 1960s was manipulated, but it wasn't true.

What I really loved about Andrew and Tony and all those people in the early 1960s is that we were making it up as we went along. Everyone thinks it was premeditated, but it so obviously wasn't. Paul McCartney, John Lennon, they didn't know what they were doing. There were people then who had masterplans and were contrived, but they weren't the artists.

I don't think anyone knew that we were going through a big cultural change. I did start to see it when I was married, because there were rules that my parents had lived by that didn't work any more. I remember thinking that it was impossible trying to do what they'd done because everything was different and that wasn't the way anyone wanted to be any more. I think I must have got nervous, promiscuity terrified me so I thought I'd better get married! And I then wanted a very normal straight family life and it was out of the question. John was taking LSD, our best friends were Terry Sullivan and Allen Ginsberg and on our honeymoon we went to Hotel Louisiana in Paris and all I remember is our friends taking these mixtures and passing out all the time, and that was it. It wasn't what I expected! And it never was going to be. And what I loved about John was that bit of him, and you have to take what you get, but it wasn't my fantasy of marriage. It was great fun but it wasn't what I wanted, or thought I wanted.

I think my girlhood was all too short. I was probably a bit too young for motherhood, although I don't know because I never knew any different. Everyone seems to think I was though. I can't have done everything wrong because I loved my baby and we're terribly close now and I never felt out of control, but I felt worried sometimes and I ended up being quite desperate with everything at one point. I hadn't started using drugs and I didn't even smoke cigarettes or drink, but I had a little child and a feckless husband and I had to work all the time to keep it going. It's not an unusual scenario at all of course, but it was hard and when I met Mick Jagger he could see that. I didn't know him very well, but he came to see me one day with Andrew. I think I'd actually thrown John out by then so I was on my own with Nicholas and a nanny, and it was winter and there was no heating. I remember seeing how deeply shocked Mick was at this perfect creature living with a small child in an unheated apartment in Knightsbridge, but we coped. I didn't think about it much. I was very tough I guess, but I must have had this air of fragility about me which I wasn't aware of, and I was quite shocked when I realised how Mick felt.

I don't really remember quite how I got into a relationship with Mick, but I can see from my old photographs that two and a half years into my life as a singer I'm obviously having gland and sinus trouble and getting colds a lot and I'm not really getting what I need, and I'm not happy. So I can't say it wasn't a relief to stop singing when I met Mick because it was. I'd worked amazingly hard in my own little way for three years and I accepted the protection of a very wealthy powerful man for a while. I think I just took it as a little breather, and then I thought I'd go on again, which was a dreadful thing to do to Mick. I never said I'd marry him or anything, it was just assumed that we would be together forever and that's what I really wanted to think. I think I needed it and I think he knew it.

So I gave up singing partly because I was tired, but I was also terribly competitive I'm afraid and really, when I saw what Mick and Keith Richards were up to with The Rolling Stones, which was basically just to conquer the world—and they did it—I just thought, oh well, I think I'll bow out for a while, I can't do anything like that. It was very bad for my confidence, and my confidence wasn't that great anyway. When I'd started it had been because I was really ignorant and terribly sure of myself, but it got very chipped away, partly because the life was very hard. I've always been somebody who falls off their perch at 11.30. I have to get eight hours sleep a day, I have to eat, I have to take a walk and I didn't know that at the time.

So I gave it all up to try and live the life of a courtesan with Mick. I didn't get feminism for ages. Of course now I understand and I think it's the one thing which really came out of the 1960s but I can't say I had anything to do with it. I mean there they were on the barricades and I couldn't give a fuck. I didn't care at all.

And it was exciting to be there in the wake of the comet of The Rolling Stones. It was very interesting and I wouldn't have missed it for anything. But I was in the classic feminine position. I was the clever beautiful woman behind the great man, and I was very useful and so was Keith's girlfriend at the time, Anita Pallenberg. We both were, for what they wanted.

The whole thing was very interesting because we were useful in the dream sense, in the sense of the archetype. To meet a woman like me for Mick Jagger and for Keith Richards to have Anita was wonderful. They had access to our minds, much more than our bodies, which is what was so interesting because we shared our dreams with them. And I didn't mind sharing my dreams. I didn't feel resentful at all.

Everything started to get really exciting around the time of the *Beggars Banquet* album in 1968 and I thought, yes, you can access my mind and my dreams, you can have it! I didn't mind because it was so fascinating. I didn't think of it as being a muse and I still don't, it was more interesting than that. I think Anita and I were the only women at the time for those two people to write those songs in that way, and that was how it was. A muse has a much more powerless role and I didn't have a powerless role, I had a very, very strong role. Everything Mick wrote I heard first and I did a lot of shaping and changing and fixing. And everything Keith wrote I heard too actually, because we were all so close.

I've never said anything about it before. People have always tried to get it out of me but I never said anything because I didn't want it to be misinterpreted, because I'm obviously not saying I even co-wrote anything. But I did have the eye and the ear to say 'You know, just shift that a little', and so did Anita and I think it irritated them. But it doesn't matter because we were right!

I also affected everything Mick read which was an extraordinary thing. I wasn't the only one, there were other people influencing him in that way too, but they would often tell me about things and I would read them and then give them to Mick. That was real sort of student stuff, but I was fascinated by it because I hadn't fulfilled myself on that level.

You must understand that I'm not saying I wrote for The Rolling Stones, but I really did write 'Sister Morphine'. It was such a beautiful tune and it was just lying around because Mick couldn't think of the words for it, and I just decided 'Oh God, I'm going to do this.' And it came out complete. I just sat down and wrote it. To give Mick credit, he was quite able to take that, probably more than Keith. It's that sort of bisexual thing you see. Andrew could cope with the feminine spirit quite well, very well, and so could Mick. Much more so than the true 'man' like Keith.

I don't think being with Mick was ever going to be a permanent state though. It was just for a few years. That was how it felt, and after that I really had to take up my own stuff and move on. And it was lucky really because eventually I was bored, and restless, and not doing anything, so I did sort of back down from that life. But I did believe and still believe that Mick was a great star and doing something extraordinary and it was astounding actually, and I hadn't expected it at all. And I wasn't ready to cope with it, I never realised I would ever be able to do anything like that myself at all. But then again I must have known or else I wouldn't have been able to stay alive. I think I did have a sort of feeling that I had some mission to fulfil. I didn't know what, but I would find out eventually and somehow it would work, but all I had to do was not die for a few years, because otherwise I wouldn't be able to do my mission.

I don't know, it was very complicated but I couldn't bear being that person I was with Mick and I did want to destroy it. It would have been a great blessing really for me and for Mick and my son Nicholas and everyone, if I had been able to glory in it and enjoy it and just do it, but I couldn't. It really, really made me feel bad. I don't blame Mick, I really don't, because he can't help the way he is, he's a star, he had a real inner power, and no, it wasn't anything to do with black magic! But what are you supposed to do? Damp yourself down? I know that women damp themselves down, but it's easier for women to do that because there's a sort of pattern for you. I mean I did it and it nearly killed me, but certainly I would never have expected somebody like that to do it for me. But I felt as if I was in a goldfish bowl and there was a lot of hatred and jealousy and envy from other women and it was really, really bad and it was a thing I didn't know how to deal with. I mean I was so young. When I left Mick to go on the street and shoot dope I think I was only 22.

Obviously the way to deal with it is to face these women down and stand up for yourself and not believe all that shit, but I couldn't do it, I believed everything. So I ended up thinking the best thing I could do was be a junkie and live on the street because that's where I belonged. And actually it was a very good idea, because I did get my anonymity back. Just having no phone number, no address, nobody knows where you are, is very, very, very healing. And all the street people were great, and they didn't know who I was, they didn't know anything about me. I was just another sort of drifter.

It was a dreadful business and I only realised years later how it must have affected Jagger. To turn down life with Mick and go and live on the street as a junkie—it's just wild! It's a horrible thing to do and I was obviously trying to say, 'That's what I think of you and your life!' It was nasty but that's the way it goes.

On another level my mind was influenced through reading William Burroughs. Mick read him too but he didn't have to go and live on the street. I took it literally. Of course Burroughs didn't do that himself, but I was sure he was saying, 'Go forth and live on the street and shoot smack!'

Of course, though, becoming a heroin addict is the worst thing for a woman to do. With men there is this great romantic tradition with Samuel Coleridge, Edgar Allen Poe, Baudelaire, there are millions of them. If you're a woman, you immediately become a whore. I used to know more about this, I've forgotten a lot because I've stopped worrying about it but I noticed it a lot when I was in Narcotics Anonymous and I was going to these meetings and it was impossible for a woman to tell her story as a drug addict and come out with any sense of bravado, or say, 'Well I had a great time' because it is the lowest thing you can do. It's lower on the scale than prostitution.

I think it's because in every way, in any tribe at all, the woman is a sacred being who is a holy place. When I was younger I didn't understand how important women are for men, how they can't do anything without women. I don't just mean have children, but the way women are so intuitive, the way they dream so much and everything is going on in there, I'm sure men aren't like that and they can't do it. They don't have that magical thing, that intuitive sense of everything, and they get it through women and women are meant to be this sacred force. And what I finally decided was that the only really big mistake you can make is to not respect your own life, and to become a heroin addict is to try and destroy yourself in a very, very serious way, there's no question about it. And if you're a woman you contaminate yourself in the eyes of humanity, and you see it very clearly now with AIDS.

Our whole job as women is to nurture, and that's why the woman addict is hated because she goes completely against that. It's much more than a stereotype or an archetype, because for the race to continue at all, women must have children who are healthy. And of course HIV comes about through intravenous drug use and sexuality and both of those things are anathema.

I must say, having done it, I don't recommend it! But it did heal me a lot and when I was better I just went to my doctor. I'd been on the National Health and getting vast amounts of dope every day, but in the end I just went to my dear Dr Willis and said, 'Well, I think I've finished now, I'd like to stop.' So he put me in a hospital in Bexley and they put me on a cure which took eight months, because I had such a vast habit. Eventually I got off, but I got back into it years later, because my healing was not complete. The street life helped me in some ways but there was a whole lot of other stuff I'd never dealt with. I did need to do all the treatment and the therapy. On the most basic level I had to stop shooting smack, and stop living on the street and come back into society and work. It was a difficult thing to do, and I didn't reintegrate, I just pretended.

The music helped. It does sound strange, almost too strange, but I'm sure you can understand that because I'd used my voice, I'd used my breathing. In the actual act of singing I was my instrument myself and I think, as I learnt later from meditation and lots of other things, that just breathing very deeply kept me alive. When I was really fucked up, in 1970, I made this awful record with Mike Leander, who had produced me earlier in my career, and it's incredibly horrible because you can hear I'm dying. I can't listen to it now.

For a long time when I was really, really dreaming up *Broken English*, I didn't sing very much, I just listened to records, and not very many either because I didn't have any money. I think I only had three or four actually, but that's what kept me alive. And then I had this hit in Ireland with 'Dreamin' My Dreams' and I went on tour again so I started to sing and that is really what got me back, it gave me the strength.

And David Bowie was helpful. He was looking for 1960s archetypes to promote his covers album *Pin Ups*. He got Marianne Faithfull back from the dead to coincide with that. He was nice to me, all it ever takes really is for someone to be nice to me and I'm fine, I cheer right up. So he put me on this television show which was recorded at The Marquee in London and was filmed by an American TV company. It was in 1973 and that was a bit before punk and it wasn't enough actually, I needed the punk energy to really do something. This was years before *Broken English*. But it was the first attention I got from anybody in that world for a long time, because I was locked in my own icy world. And I would go to concerts occasionally and it was impossible. What David did was take the trouble to take his pick axe and hack through the stone to get to me, to get me to do something. But I think it was Angie, his wife, who really told him to go and find me.

But it was punk which really interested me, and sort of got me going again. I loved the Sex Pistols, especially John Lydon. I didn't really know them, although I shared the same drug dealer as Sid Vicious! But the energy from punk really did help with the making of *Broken English*, and so did my husband at the time, Ben Brierley, although he ended up loathing me for it because he was eclipsed by its success. But if I hadn't made it I would have cut my throat, and that is the truth. It was so fucking serious.

Really I would have been delighted if someone else had made something like *Broken English* because then I wouldn't have had to do it. I waited for years thinking I wouldn't have to bother, but there was nothing going on that I wanted to hear musically. The 1970s were dead musically—apart from punk of course. Everything was on such a huge scale and I wasn't interested. So eventually I realised I would have to make *Broken English*, and then of course everyone was shocked by the change in me.

Everyone thought I was an angel when I was young, but I've had very little patience with that stuff. People who knew me in the 1960s looked at me with amazement and horror when *Broken English* came out, and they still do now, because I don't look now like I looked then. I look now like I wished I'd looked then. It's true, I remember what I wanted to look like then and now I do! But it took a long time, I had to smoke a lot and do all that other stuff first. And that's how I got the voice, and that's the important thing, not how I looked. I eventually got the voice that was able to express my inner state so that people would know who I really was, and it was a tough call. If I'd gone into opera or something, I could have used that beautiful high voice in another way, but I went into the wrong medium with it and I couldn't fake it, there was no way I could have done it. I would have loved to have been able to sing the blues when I was 17, but I couldn't do it, it wasn't natural.

After *Broken English* everyone started saying I was a survivor and at the time I was incredibly irritated by that. When I came back into the world I was incredibly sensitive, especially after using dope. I mean I really was, it was very easy to get to me. If you just said anything I could hardly take it. And it seemed amazingly unfair to me that after everything I'd been through that all people had to say was that I was a survivor because there was so much more I was trying to do.

Of course there must have been a time when all I had to do was survive, but it went much further than that, I had a mission, and I think it's really been difficult for people to accept that. I was a very light being when I started and I really am too now, you can see. It's got its own depth, but it's very out there, spinning away, light, it's not heavy, and I've always been like that, and it's made people think I wasn't serious because I play, but that's how it is.

And I was really astounded actually when I did *Broken English* because it was such a momentous thing to do. It was like this global thing and it really got people, especially some of the critics who reviewed it. Nicholas remembers it well, he was about 15, and I remember too, particularly Charles Shaar Murray's review in *NME*. It was really vicious and bitter and angry and vituperative. Lots of women reviewed it too, but why do you think the reviews by men were more bitter? Let's throw it open. Because of the jealousy and the guilt maybe, the guttural cry of it. Men romanticise female pain, like, 'Oh, this one must have been really hurt by something.'

The vibe I get from the way men write about women now is like, 'Look, this thing's gone far enough. Women have got so much freedom, it's ridiculous! It has to stop!' There's this kind of feeling that now it's men who are oppressed! I've actually relaxed a bit and started thinking, 'Oh God, who cares anymore, let's stop worrying about it.' But at the moment I'm not under direct fire. And I will be.

I never used to have any idea about how desperate men are to understand women and now I see it all the time, everywhere I look, and it really hurts me. They're trying to make a deal to somehow get to understand because they don't understand why women are angry or what's going on, what women are feeling. But in a way I don't think they really want to, it's all too much for them. That's why it's such a hard thing to actually be in a relationship and go through it and, I'm sorry to say this, just the thought of training somebody to understand what you are and who are and what you mean is just too much for me. It takes 10 years and then they might not get it anyway. And it is like that. And yet we get a lot from them too, I suppose.

What's really irritating is that people think if you do something extraordinary, there must be some guy in the background pulling the strings. And it's funny, but I have to say that we do still need the patriarchy to get by, and I did notice that doing my last record. And I'm crazy sometimes with that and I have had the feeling that I've been in tremendous peril because the patriarchy wasn't going to let me get what I wanted out, and I've really had to go through some scenes. It's like a game, you have to continually make your moves. The producer is always a man, in my case anyway, and they have the power and they get the money. And I have to deal with that.

When I was doing *Broken English* I played a tape of Heathcote Williams reading his lyrics to 'Why D'Ya Do It?' for the band, and they were so shocked and stunned because they thought I was a lady and they said, 'You're not going to do that.' I couldn't believe it. I said, 'Yes I am and you're going to play it!' And I suppose this is where women get the reputation for being bitches. When a woman takes her will and forces it onto a group of men, they react by saying, 'This person is a bitch.' There's a force in them which is very frightened of the true feminine spirit.

The fact that music is providing women with their own particular forms of expression is very new really. The bands that are doing this work haven't been doing it for long. When I started it was a very male-dominated world. I hate these phrases like 'male-dominated', but it was, and it's very recently that it seems that the world has opened up to women because really what people like best is either women singing or men who sound like women singing. And they have liked men who sound like women singing for a long time. I think that was always the charm of people like Mick and David Bowie, they were very on the edge, the whole thing was very blurred. And what these young girl bands are doing now is taking over that territory.

It's still pretty limited for women in some ways though. It made me really angry when Patti Smith's *Dream of Life* record was rejected. She changed her opinions and fell in love and got married and had kids and made a tender record and her record was rejected because she wasn't the raging junkie anymore. I don't know her that well, but I know she was incredibly hurt by that. It seems that if it isn't the old stereotype, then it's got to be another stereotype and you're not allowed to change your mind. You're really not meant to. I'm afraid to say that I think we have a problem with the humanity of women, and that this is not recognised. Women are not really allowed to be human beings. Men can change their minds and it's OK. Also, it seems to be that there is a range of emotion for women to feel. You're either allowed to be sappy and romantic, and I don't mean romanticism is sappy, I mean Mills and Boon kind of romance, or you're allowed to be angry and vicious, but you're not allowed to express the other things. And that's exactly what I'm trying to do with my new record but I don't know what people will think and honestly I don't particularly care.

The whole thing is on the run really. What about that man in Gloucester who was accused of killing all those girls this year? The hatred men have for women is unbelievable. But the other side of that is the love they have, which is very intense too. They adore us. But they can't bear to be out of control and love us that much, they really can't bear it. And to be hated for what you are and who you are, just because you're a woman, to be hated so much that people will kill you and bury you under cement! But we can't change our sex, and I don't want to, I love being a woman.

I had bought the direct picture that men despised women, and some do but most of them don't. Most of them adore women, they just worship us and they'll do anything for us. But worshipping doesn't really help because all you want is to be treated like another human being. Although I wouldn't mind a bit of worship now. When you're my age you think, oh all right, if you want to worship me I'll let you! But it certainly didn't cover the bases for me when I was young, I wanted much more. But what do you do? You could become gay of course. I always think that would be the best thing. If only I could really go in for it properly, but I can't quite get it and I know that would be the way but I don't want to. I like men. I don't want to shut them out.

I went to a knicker shop today. It was this wonderful shop in Knightsbridge. I used to go there in the 1960s and I was wondering who would like the stuff in there now. The assistants were showing me these beautiful things with holes in the right places, and obviously either prostitutes or your man who's done a bit of time in jail love all that. I know they do. And rock stars. I asked the assistants, did men buy them for women, and they said yes. But not many men would go into Bradleys and say, 'I want a pair of crotchless knickers for my wife.' They wouldn't. And their wives probably wouldn't. I mean, I don't think I could buy something like that. Well I could, and I have done it, but I don't think I could do it now. Maybe it's because of my age, but it would frighten a man terribly bringing back a pair of knickers like that. Because it means something. It means I know this relationship is sexual and I accept it and now what? Do it! And that creates tremendous pressure, I mean we all act as if it's not a big deal, taking the initiative, but buying a pair of crotchless knickers is definitely taking the initiative! Then again I might be wrong, but I think they'd be very frightened that you were a slut. If you were prepared to go that far, what else would you do?

So there's no question that men are somewhat on the run. They're pretty frightened because we've all got much more assertive and much clearer about what we want sexually and I think I might have missed that in a way, and I still haven't managed it, to say, 'Now look dear, this is what I like.' But I know that the younger generations of women are all completely able to do that. It's very important and I'm from another time and I found it very hard. It's a very personal thing, and I'm sure you couldn't do it with a one night stand. With a one night stand you get what you get, but they can be wonderful! We all know that!

Credentials

Signed to: Decca 1964–1969, NEMS 1975–1978, Island Records 1979–present

Managed by: Art Collins

Select discography: *Come My Way* LP (1965)

Marianne Faithfull LP (1965)

North Country Maid LP (1966)

Love In A Mist LP (1967)

The World of Marianne Faithfull LP (1969)

Dreamin' My Dreams LP (1977)

Rich Kid Blues LP (1978)

Broken English LP (1979)

Dangerous Acquaintances LP (1981)

A Child's Adventure LP (1983)

Strange Weather LP (1987)

Blazing Away live LP (1990)

Faithfull LP (1994)

Kim Gordon

'*All* these guys writing about music only seem to like women who sing nice little melodies and pop princesses, and I know those loser writers with bad teeth at 26, and where are they going in life? Where will they be when they're my age?'

Kim Gordon

Introduction

With her band Sonic Youth, Kim Gordon has risen out of New York's underground scene and achieved cult status in Britain and America. Over the last decade or so her cool, blonde strength has helped diffuse the usually male aggression of guitar rock into more balanced realms and she has become something of a role model for girls now breaking into music. Her songs are littered with sensual whispers of desire, ironic parodies of teenage talk, tales of enigmatic female characters living on the outback of subcultures and day to day women's issues, undercutting the boy rock stance of her male contemporaries with a whole range of female perspectives and integrating them into the spectrum of her otherwise all-male band.

By her own admission a model child until the age of 12, Gordon graduated in fine art and moved from the commercially competitive atmosphere of Los Angeles to the more artistic world of New York where she found work. More intrigued with ideas than their expression, she eventually grew frustrated with art theory and became more attracted to connecting directly with popular culture through music.

Gordon formed Sonic Youth with Thurston Moore, the musician whom she later married (and with whom she now has a daughter, Coco Hayley Gordon Moore) and the band initially built up a reputation on the New York new wave art rock scene of the early 1980s. At the end of the decade they moved onto a major record label and became known as mentors of guitar rock after introducing Nirvana to their management company, thus helping to instigate the Seattle trio's phenomenal success. Gordon and Moore now advise their label on up and coming bands, on a semi-official basis.

In addition to Sonic Youth, Gordon has involved herself in a number of projects, including Velvet Underground drummer Moe Tucker's solo record, *Life In Exile After Abdication* and a tribute album to Californian writer Harry Crews with performance art activist, writer and erstwhile musician, Lydia Lunch, titled *Naked In Garden Hills*. She has also co-directed two of The Breeders' videos, co-produced Courtney Love's band Hole's debut album, *Pretty On The Inside* and plays in Free Kitten with her friend Julie Cafritz, formerly of New York underground supremos, Pussy Galore. Most recently Gordon has launched a clothes label, X Girl, with Julie's sister Daisy, and has opened a shop in Los Angeles selling garments for all body types.

Still making relevant rock music at the age of 41, Gordon is challenging society's perceptions of 'older' women. She has refused to mellow with time and has consequently been criticised for it by the British music press who have hounded her for not 'acting her age' and dubbed her with condescending titles such as 'Riot Grran' and 'Den Mother'. While Gordon appreciates the crossover between rock and youth cultures, she believes she has more to offer younger people than many of the older male artists who are treated more respectfully.

In fact, Gordon has always been very much in touch with youth culture and is scornful of the lack of understanding afforded by the media to young female rock activity. When Riot Grrl, the action-based, anti-establishment feminist upsurge of 1992 exploded, Gordon spoke out in support and has since befriended members of the Grrl affiliated band, Bikini Kill. She has also been openly supportive of abortion rights in America, appearing in a public service announcement in 1991 and performing at Rock For Choice benefits with Free Kitten.

Gordon's feminist concerns translate visually as well as sonically and politically. Trashing the more theatrical trappings of her field, she concentrates on appearing as 'normal' as possible in order to demystify the glamour of entertainment and presents herself very much as she is. The one time she did dress up was in 1990 for *Goo*, Sonic Youth's first major label album, which she described as their 'pop record', and the mood was very tongue in cheek. Usually her style is subtle, being more of a personal expression than a cry for attention. This is probably what inspired international clothing line The Gap to use Gordon's picture in one of their highly successful black and white 'individual interpretation' advertisements.

Now an undisputed force in popular culture, having maintained her connections with the art world and broken through into video, Gordon is also expanding into film and has written her first script for a teen movie about a girl band, with director Tamra Davis. Together with her continuing career as Sonic Youth's bass player, Gordon's ventures prove her to be an increasingly relevant multimedia artist, who thankfully refuses to grow older quietly.

Kim Gordon

I grew up in Los Angeles and my background was pretty middle class family life. I was a model child until I was 12 and then I decided to be bad! My older brother who I looked up to was bad. He was very mean to me and he later became schizophrenic in his early twenties, and really, you know, paranoid schizophrenic, he was really hostile.

Anyway, I was very precocious for my age. Recently I was talking with Thurston because we were thinking of names for the baby, and when we found out it was going to be a girl, we were thinking of Lolita and I thought, oh God my mother would die! She gave that book *Lolita* by Vladimir Nabokov to me when I was 12 because she was afraid I was going to turn out like the character Lolita or something. I think it was really odd for her to give me that book when I was so young but I think she was trying to stress that you can be one kind of girl or another. She made it so black and white, you know, like if you read and you're more intellectual then men will like you a lot and not just for your body. She was trying to teach me something like that. I was always a tomboy, I never wore little dresses or anything and I was fairly independent so she was just more afraid I think, because I was so sexually precocious and mature for my age that she was scared I'd get pregnant by the time I was 13.

Ever since I was little I'd been doing art. I always had private art classes and stuff and I graduated in fine art, which was post-conceptual. In my final year at art school, there was this guy who was involved with a band called Airport or something. It was just a noise tunnel in a warehouse full of airplane propellers—it was just noise, but I had this feeling that what he was doing was more interesting than everything else that was going on. I mean he had this reputation for being a cutting edge art student, but when he started making music I was like, 'What's up with that!'

To me the idea is more important than how you express it, and I was interested in the kinds of art that made comments about popular culture, and towards the end of my work with art I was thinking about female expression in relation to things like ad copy. You used to get these ads using a first-person sentence, like the swimsuit ads with the big type saying things like 'I feel like a million dollars.' I would take the ad and sign my name to it and put it in another magazine. I was sort of starting to get into that but in a way there was such a backlash to feminist art when I was doing it. There were all these really strong women around like Cindy Sherman, Sherrie Levine and Jenny Holzer but Cindy's was the only work which related directly to being a woman. If you wanted to compete, your work had to be intellectually there more than it should have been. It was like, if your work seemed too feminist-oriented people wouldn't take it seriously on an intellectual cutting edge level. I was sort of drifting away from it interest-wise by then. And I wanted to take the popular culture thing further, I wanted to take it one step further than Andy Warhol so eventually it made more sense for me to work within a genre that related more directly to that, like music.

With art I think I was too intellectual about it. I think I was paralysed with knowing too much, whereas music I really don't know anything about. And I think that music is definitely more emotionally fulfilling than art. Art has to be more about ideas rather than some emotional outlet of expressionistic painting or something. Even though I'm a very physical person and I like the act of painting, it's very enjoyable to me but it's not satisfying, just the physicalness alone. And that was always a big conflict for me because it was something that I grew up doing all my life and I liked the physicality of it but when I started learning about all these art ideas I couldn't resolve the two together. And I think that's why I like playing music because it's really physical as well. Doing art is very lonely and depressing!

There's nothing I like better than to talk about ideas with some artist friends of mine, and I usually only talk to artist friends about certain kinds of ideas because other people may think you're being pretentious or something. But it's a challenge to me to integrate certain ideas into popular culture with music or with things that might apply them more directly like videos or songs, and the thing I like about writing songs and singing is that it's almost like taking on different personalities, it's almost like acting.

I'll always be visually oriented because that's how I think. I don't think musically really. When I think musically, I think in terms of soft or loud, in contrasts, because I don't know anything about notes. I personally never wanted to play traditional rock anyway. I don't think a lot of women want to. Women are less exposed to that than men, they don't go through the same teenage rituals as boys do, sitting in their bedrooms and listening to records and copying lead guitarists. It's not that women can't do that, it's just that I think most of them don't want to.

I never wanted to play the bass in a conventional way, or the guitar. There was never any reason for me to learn because in Sonic Youth, we always made music by listening to each other. Lee and Thurston were always on weird tunings anyway, so it made more sense to work things out by listening. There is a certain jock mentality to technique in music. I certainly associate the two, and to me it's just boring. It's like a workout, a display of virtuosity.

When I first came to New York I formed a band called CKM with my friends Christine and Miranda. CKM stood for our names, and we got together for this Dan Graham performance art piece. Dan had a mirror behind him, and he would face the audience and describe them, and then he would turn around and describe himself describing the audience. He did all these weird things and he wanted an all-girl band to do a show with him.

So we had a song called 'Soft Posh Separates' which was like the ads for clothes you mix and match together, and we had songs about lipstick. We were kind of making fun of girl talk. There was one song called 'Cosmopolitan Girl', based on this series of ads *Cosmopolitan* magazine did. I took the lyrics from the ads and made up a song from it!

The performance was sort of screwed up though. We were all supposed to do something after each song but Miranda left to go to the bathroom! After that we never played together again. But Miranda introduced me to Thurston, who was playing with The Coachmen, and we got together. We started playing music with this other girl and then we met Lee. Thurston came up with the name Sonic Youth and as soon as we had a name it took direction.

Sometimes it's awkward, being in a band with my husband, but it's what we've always known. You don't want to alienate the other people in the band by making them feel like you're this couple, and that you become powerful because there's two of you. But Thurston and I don't always agree on things, and I'm always aware that I spend too much time worrying or caring about what other people think. The older I get, the less I really care about it!

Some people like to exploit their relationships with their husbands but I've never really been into that because I like to feel like I'm an individual. I think it's more important to fight to be yourself in that way but Thurston's a Leo, so he has a natural leader-type quality and you can't fight that! The biggest problem is being on stage if Thurston's having a bad time technically. He's got better at it, but he used to really freak out and when you're so sensitive to somebody's moods, it's kind of hard. You have to learn to ignore it because otherwise it can be really nerve-racking!

Being in a band with men can get boring though. I'm sort of used to being around men because I was a tomboy, but there are some really boring aspects to it, like when they just want to talk about records or whatever. I mean I know a few girls who collect records, but for the most part it seems to be a sport. Playing with Julie in Free Kitten is so different because we're best friend. Communication-wise it's different, it's generally easier. You understand things like photographs!

It's weird though because when it's just the two of us in Kitten it's not a gender issue at all, but when we've played with Yoshimi from The Boredoms, suddenly it's three GIRLS. And what are we? Shonen Knife? When we played with Mark from Pavement it was fun, it wasn't a gender thing, it was just another personality in the band. We joked around, degrading him, but it wasn't a big deal.

I also found it weird doing the Harry Crews tour with Lydia Lunch and Sadie Mae. Lydia kind of wanted to exploit Sadie's dumbness in a typical male way. And both of them had these incredibly loud, dirty mouths. Me and the tour manager would be in the van going, 'Ohhh!' I felt weird, like there was something wrong with me for not bonding with these women, but I felt alienated from both of them.

So I like being in a band with men for the most part. Although sometimes it's hard because no matter how much of a new man someone thinks they are, they're just not! There's always some prejudice there. I think that in general there's a preconception about indie rock, that it's not sexist and that it's very accepting of women, but I see the mainstream of it as pretty conservative, like college rock or something. There's a certain competitiveness and when people feel competitive, they feel more threatened. So there are boys who say bands like Bikini Kill can't play, and the English press are always saying it about Huggy Bear, and they just don't get it. They don't understand what's really sophisticated about it, so if you're a girl band you're forced into being pop or being rock, because otherwise you think people won't take you seriously. And it seems like there are less girls making experimental music for that reason.

There is a drive to be accepted, even Bikini Kill had their girl rock anthem, which makes total sense if you want to get your message across. So what's more important, the medium or the message?

I see Free Kitten as being more experimental, I guess. A lot of people don't take us seriously because I'm in Sonic Youth and Julie was in Pussy Galore, so they try and call us a joke band or a supergroup or a side project. I mean, do you have to have a career at everything? In a certain way it makes it less valid if it isn't a career I guess, but how many pop songs actually change people's lives? Maybe you just like a song and it feels good, but it doesn't change your life, so what's the validity in justifying something by saying that it reaches a lot of people? I think Huggy Bear are probably just having a good time, which is definitely as important as anything.

I choose to play with Julie because we have similar tastes, and we're friends and we want it to be fun. But I wouldn't go out of my way to start an all-girl band, because one of the irritating things about the media is the way they judge you. When Riot Grrl exploded, girl bands were judged on how Riot Grrl they were. And me and Julie were criticised because the only girl-oriented song on our *Straight Up* record was 'Dick', and that song changes every time we play it. You can't win, it's just another way for men to control the media.

The problem is that there are only three or four clichéd personalities you can be as far as the media is concerned. With men the range is greater. They can just be boys. It's like, 'Oh isn't he cute, he's just a boy, he can't help it, girls like him.' Where do you ever see 'Oh she's just a girl'? That would probably be insulting to most women anyway! But unless you're overtly making yourself into a freak like Siouxsie Sioux, unless you have a really strong, stereotypical role to put yourself in, you come across as all too human and the media can't deal with it.

In England especially, I've always found men to be very ambivalent. It's very odd, but they seem afraid. I've read interviews and reviews of Sonic Youth where the guy writing has been subtly hostile towards me, making me out to be the bad one or making me out to be invisible, like just not wanting to deal with me. It makes sense because the Queen is almost like a transvestite you know, and there's such a huge trend of homosexual English male pop stars. I always feel very uncomfortable in England.

It's the same idea with lyrics. It's hard for people to figure out why some girls sing about things and other girls sing about other things, and really it's so simple. It's just to do with different personalities and what interests them. That's why I've always tried to be as ordinary as possible, because for me it's really important for some other girl to see that I don't have to be a freak or a drug addict or have a Siouxsie Sioux persona and I can still be creative, and I can still express myself in a powerful way—just by being myself.

I think your songs are based so much on your personality and that hasn't really been acknowledged yet. Kathleen Hanna of Bikini Kill writes the songs she does partly because of her personality, in the same way I do. And that has to allow for change. Certainly I'm a different person, somewhat, to what I was. I've always been angry and rebellious, but I was never raunchy, it just wasn't part of my personality. The same as I never really said things to shock people, although I always liked confrontation. So with Sonic Youth my lyrics have sometimes been weird psychological things, and sometimes more direct and sometimes more like stories.

We have written songs from a definite female viewpoint, like 'Flower' in 1985. And 'Kool Thing', which was a single from the *Goo* album in 1990 which I wanted to be taken literally, like you know, 'Please liberate me from corporate white male oppression'. It was also about having really ridiculous expectations about pop stars you idolise like LL Cool J. Did Jane Fonda get involved with leftist politics because she lusted after the Black Panther? It was about how no one ever talks about white women being intrigued by anarchist, rebellious types, like an extension of the James Dean bad boy rebel thing, on another level, an alternative to the white male, because white women are all too familiar with that kind of power. Also in the 1960s, feminists were called the niggers of the left because no one really wanted to consider them. They just wanted these girls to hang around and be pretty and not speak too much.

'Shadow Of A Doubt' from the *Evol* album is more like a story but the character is female. Have you ever met someone who just looks at you and gives you shivers up and down your spine because they're sort of creepy? Their eyes just go into you, it's the equivalent of them undressing you with their eyes. And then you have this déjà vu feeling about how earlier in your life, when you were little, you had the same sort of creepy feeling for someone or something. Maybe it happens to boys too, I don't know! But I was trying to get that feeling across.

We've written a lot about female icons too, in one way or another. Like with 'Tunic (Song for Karen)' on *Goo* which was kind of about Karen Carpenter. She was so symbolic of a lot of women in America with bad self-image problems, and that meant her voice had this incredible vulnerability to it, in the midst of all that really schlocky music. In retrospect, in relation to her life, her lyrics were tragically profound. And you can really hear it in her voice. She was really repressed, she was controlled and the only control she had was over her body. She never had a life of her own, she'd played adult music since she was a teenager, and she didn't leave home until really late, despite the fact that she was making money.

Some women have control over their bodies by making themselves into sex symbols, like Madonna. Madonna is sort of trapped because she's become such a freak. She's completely lost the human element, and that probably began when she started exercising.

There's a song on the new record which comes from looking at those Guess? jeans ads and fantasising about how I'd feel if I were looking at those ads as a young girl. I'm supposed to be relating to Drew Barrymore and I start fantasising about the ad and the guy in the ad. It's not really sexual, it's more like a girl, self-image thing.

Female icons in our culture are always sort of passive. They're really like these vessels. What is a sexual object? Well, it's something that's passive, to be looked at or thought about, and sexual objects evoke action or reaction in other people, but they don't necessarily have much action themselves. You know it's all passive manipulation. So in writing about them, we're allowing ourselves to be passively manipulated and seeing where it takes us I guess.

I think that images of women in popular culture can have a tremendous effect on the way people think about women though. When Madonna was younger, there were all those Madonna wannabes, although I don't know if they got the message of sexual power—that sex is OK, or whether it was just a fashion statement. But certainly having someone like Hillary Clinton in the White House has made a huge difference in the kind of message that it gives out to society, like we've come into modern life, and we have a family there who reflect the culture here.

I don't know about the visual importance of female images in popular culture though, because if you look at that whole waif thing and those pictures that Corinne Day took, they actually weren't about a new look and skinny models. It was all supposed to be an anti-fashion statement. It was about the girls' personalities being stripped down, they weren't posing or flaunting their sexuality in a conventional way. But it was packaged to become a new kind of sexuality, the new androgyny or whatever. That's the thing about advertising and packaging in popular culture, it's hard to escape. It's hard to retain a private quality and get the essence of that private quality across and have it retain whatever it was that made it interesting for you in the first place.

Certainly when you're making a video it's hard because you have to accept the format, that basically you're making an advertisement. But there are certain traditional ways in which women are presented to the camera which interest me, like submissive camera angles. Hopefully you can use them with a sense of irony, but it is hard.

Part of the big sell in Western culture is the youth issue. Eastern cultures know all about the life cycle and ageing, but in this culture everyone is so afraid of death. We don't incorporate death into our living, intellectually or anything.

People don't quite know how old I am. If you're in the entertainment business it makes it much harder! It's weird because I guess you always think of yourself as being a certain age, no matter how old you are. But there've been some really mean things written about me. I mean, what kind of music am I supposed to play now? Am I just supposed to turn into another type of person? Nobody knows what you do when you get to this age. Patti Smith, who probably started out in music the same time I did, retired. She had a baby and she found God which was a good out for her. But what do you do if you don't find God?!

All these guys writing about music only seem to like women who sing nice little melodies and pop princesses, and I know those loser writers with bad teeth at 26, and where are they going in life? Where will they be when they're my age?

I was going to make a list of all the men in bands I know who are in their thirties. It seems like unless you're Mick Jagger or Keith Richards they don't make a deal about your age. But there are older musicians like Eric Clapton who are enjoying second careers now and although I'm glad they can make a living out of it, I don't want to have to read about them or watch them getting these big awards because they're really not that good. And you have to think about the age group voting for those people, they must all be the same age group as the musicians. So I can understand the resentment on the part of kids in their twenties because that music is pretty much crap. But you have to discriminate, and I think I have just as much to offer young people, probably more so, than most people their age. What makes it interesting is the exchange between younger and older people, rather than bands where everyone is the same age and the same sex.

No one bases Neil Young's music on his age, they just say he's getting better. He is able to make music that's still relevant, and his voice carries the same integrity and he hasn't tried to make himself into the 1990s, and I think there is a real place for that authenticity in the culture, but it is disappearing. And so far I've just not been treated with the same dignity as someone of Neil Young's age, and I'm not even as old as him!

Obviously men don't like to see women ageing, because of the maternal thing with the female body. It doesn't bother me that I'm ageing because I feel better and better about myself the older I get. It's just difficult when what you do is part of the youth culture and the thing that makes me angry is all the double standards. Maybe men get more insecure as they get older, that must be it. And women come into their sexual peak in their forties! For me, everything was always so hard when I was younger and it just seems like things are coming more easily now, things are starting to open up more.

I really liked meeting Kathleen and Tobi from Bikini Kill because I really thought that they weren't that interested in me, because I'm from another generation and I'm older and they're just so into their thing and they seemed so confident and as if they didn't really care about what I thought. But then I found out that they wanted to know why I wasn't supporting them, and that they felt no one else cared about their band that much. I mean, I feel privileged that I get to meet people because of who I am. I tend to be more paranoid that people are going to resent me, that they won't want to admit their influence or that it's not sort of cool. I think it's to do with the way that rock culture's set up. It's all so much about being cool, that people would rather say they're influenced by some more unlikely person.

Anyway, as old as I am, I really feel immature, which is why I've left having a kid until now. I kind of left it 'til the last minute. I would just hate it if I didn't take advantage of the fact that I'm a woman and I can do this and there's this other side of experience for me. I was always freaked out about if I had a baby, would I start to write songs about being a mother, like Joni Mitchell? Actually I loved Joni Mitchell when I was younger, but I was worried that I'd start to write bad songs if I became a mother! But I can't worry about that any more. My other fear was I didn't want to be a housewife, and I used to get so depressed when I saw middle-class women pushing a baby stroller. But there are different ways of doing things, and besides, Thurston will make a great father!

Credentials

Bands:	Sonic Youth, Free Kitten
Sonic Youth signed to:	SST 1982–1983, Blast
	First 1985–1989, Geffen 1990–present
Free Kitten signed to:	Pearl Necklace Records
Sonic Youth managed by:	John Silva for Gold Mountain
	Entertainment
Past bands:	CKM

Select Sonic Youth discography:

Sonic Youth LP (1982)

Confusion Is Sex LP (1983)

Bad Moon Rising LP (1985)

'Flower' single (1985)

Evol LP (1986)

Sister LP (1987)

Daydream Nation LP (1988)

The Whitey Album LP (As Ciccone Youth—1989)

Goo LP (1990)

Dirty LP (1992)

Experimental Jet Set, Trash and No Star LP (1994)

Select Free Kitten discography:

Boxed EP (1994)

'*Women* are the ones who will create the balance of the world structure. Women know that to be completely ecstatic or to have a really good time you need to form close relationships with other people. Men have to learn things that women have known for centuries.'

Toni Halliday

Driven by a raging ambition to kickstart the foundations of rock traditions into accepting the hard challenge of inner female glamour and confrontational assertiveness, Toni Halliday has burnt more than just fingers with her steely attitude. Her imaginative understanding of charismatic power boots the easily-accessible surface appeal of conventional female allure offstage, replacing it with depth, intrigue and individuality, while lyrically she embraces female emotional and sexual turmoil. Music has liberated Halliday, although her studied, stark magnetism was immediately toppled into the 'ice maiden' bracket, when she found herself hailed as the new sex queen of indie rock, heaped in mystery and presented in formidable terms. Halliday is annoyed by the misunderstandings which have greeted her, but has refused to play herself down and remains unnervingly honest in her quest to be the kind of hero women want, instead of another symbol of male desire.

After an idyllic hippy childhood, Halliday was abandoned in Greece by her father at the age of seven, with her mother and sisters, and grew up, hurt and confused, in England's Northeast. At 14 she signed her first solo record deal and started modelling in the hope of raising enough money to move to London. A television appearance led to a meeting with Dave Stewart, who was then in The Tourists with her idol, Annie Lennox, and who was to prove instrumental in her musical career.

By the time she was 16 Halliday was waitressing in London and soon had another record deal with her band, The Uncles. After one single release they broke up and she joined State of Play with Dean Garcia, former Eurythmics bassist whom she'd met through Stewart, and Garcia's girlfriend Julie. Eventually Halliday was kicked out of the band, and ended up with another solo deal on Stewart's record label, Anxious, although by the time her album was released she had lost interest.

The idea for Curve came to Halliday while she was in Los Angeles with her boyfriend Alan Moulder, who was producing Shakespears Sister's album, *Hormonally Yours*. She rushed back to England, contacted Garcia, made a demo, gave it to Stewart who was duly impressed, and Curve was born. With their first EP, *Blindfold*, they sent the music press into raptures, although Halliday was quickly homed in on, becoming a focal point for itchy teenage male lust and her self-assertion was interpreted as a kind of sexy standoffishness.

With Curve behind her and a new project titled Bud underway, Halliday continues to shrug off her haughty diva image with philosophical calm. Her fascination with adornment, reinvention and masks stems from a deep interest in self-expression, not a superficial yearning to be the most beautiful face on a magazine cover. Unafraid of wearing false eyelashes with a filthy old T-shirt, Halliday embodies individual choice, while the maelstrom of emotions stirred up by her headstrong stance proves she is undeniably in control. While such a combination may fuel the fantasies of some, it's a reality in most women that men are slowly learning to have to deal with.

Toni Halliday

In Her Own Words

usic was my escape. I suppose I first remember my mum and dad on our boat in the South of France or in Greece playing music. I must have been about four or five, and my dad had this acoustic guitar and he was really bad at it. But still, music conjured up all these happy memories, of me lying in my bunk and hearing my mum and dad and their friends playing songs after they'd had a few drinks. I suppose that was the one thing that I dragged through with me from that time. Because my father left when I was seven and from that point we lost our mother. She shut down emotionally and I couldn't accept it at all, I became Joan of Arc, and I never took my armour off again because the hurt was so immense.

The fact that I never even got to ask my father why he left makes me furious. I can't handle indecision in my life at all now, a rash comes out on my body about it, and life is full of indecision. But I can't live with fear. Up until my father left we'd been living on the boat all over the place, he showed us heaven, and then he just took it all away without any explanation, and I went through a really prolonged grieving process at the loss of that intimacy.

We were abandoned in Greece with no money and my mother had to go to the Embassy to get us home. In 1972 they didn't just give you a plane ticket, you had a train ticket here, a bus ticket there and we travelled all the way back to Washington Newtown in England in that manner. It took a week and the whole thing was a bloody nightmare from the word go.

When we first got back I didn't go to school. I didn't want to cope with that, I was sick of coping. I was completely and utterly heartbroken and in total grief and I didn't want to know. And so when I actually went to school, which I had to eventually, I learnt to read and write and add up but by the time I was 11 I just switched off. There was nothing those people could teach me. I'd been there, I'd done it, and not just in an academic learning sense. What hurt could they have shown me that would have been greater than that which I'd already experienced? I was a highly sceptical child.

It was difficult for me to accept my mother as an individual and I went through years of totally blaming her for not being there for us on any emotional level. Her shutdown indicated to me that our father was more important to her than we were, so what was our existence about? Had she had us purely for our father? Loads of big questions came into play about this, but I honestly don't feel that it's any different really from the majority of people's upbringings. I think that a lot of people have had really similar experiences.

I still haven't quite come to terms with it yet though, but I am trying. I'm a classic distancer, I just isolate myself from any fear or hurt or guilt, but you never realise that you carry it with you when you run. When I was 15, I thought I'd got away with it, because I ran like a motherfucker out of Washington, but it got to the point where I wasn't behaving properly. I was totally and utterly overfunctioning, and that's why music really was my escape.

Of course it was more than just an escape. Before I left home, I managed to get a record deal, and I started thinking that this was something that was so far deep down inside of me that I knew if I had it I wouldn't need anything else.

I was lucky that punk happened because you didn't have to be any fucking good and I just dived into this swimming pool and got into my first band, Incest. I was 13 and somebody once wrote about us and said that I acted like a girl who doesn't want to be kissed at the bus stop and I thought, yeah, that's me! I was getting on my trip of how to save myself even then.

I didn't feel like the girls in my town, and half my rebellion was to do with not wanting to be like them, rather than wanting to be like me. When it comes down to it, I could quite happily have had children at 18 or 20. It's in my nature and it probably would have been OK. Björk had a child really young and it hasn't hindered her in the slightest. And look at Neneh Cherry. It's a myth, that you can't do anything with a kid. If you've got baggage from your first family, then it's a scary thing because you think, am I going to be a repeat offender, and that's what I thought.

Anyway, Incest didn't last long and I ended up with a solo deal which totally ripped me off, but at least it gave me some confidence and it led to my meeting with Dave Stewart. I'd appeared on this television programme called *Check It Out* and a *Melody Maker* journalist did a piece on me, and quoted me on Annie Lennox. At the time everyone hated her, but I was always struck by her voice and her image. I never noticed anyone else in the band, I'd never come across anyone like her before. I was an obsessive fan, I'd just stare at her because she was so stunning.

Dave and Annie read the article and he came up to Sunderland on his way to Newcastle to see his mum, and I met him in this cafe. Annie had gone on to Aberdeen, but it had been her who'd got Dave to call me in the first place. It was at the time that his lung was about to collapse, and he had a filthy cold and he was sitting there sniffling. I thought he was a junkie!

My relationship with Dave was never sexual. People have made those assumptions because they don't think it's possible to have a relationship with a man that isn't sexual. But he was with Annie then, and I was only 15 and he must have been 26 or 28. My mum had told me never to sleep with anyone in the business anyway, because it's a really small world and everyone knows everyone, and it's not worth it. Dave just wanted to look after me, he wanted to take me under his wing. He didn't help with the music at all, he just took a liking to me. He most probably saw something of himself in me because I did have incredible energy. I was really bubbly and really up. I was just about to explode and I think he saw that, and thought it was really glowing and naïve and perfect in its naïveté. And he suggested I move to London.

So I got on a train with £10 and left to do music and to totally reinvent myself. Nobody knew me in London and I could start again. I was the new strong Toni Halliday and everything else became irrelevant.

The music business is swimming with people who create their own alter egos: Bono, Chrissie Hynde, Annie Lennox. It's all about self-protection, so that nobody ever gets to the real you. But you never learn enough, you never know enough about how to protect yourself.

You find, with a lot of women who work for a living, that their yin and yang is completely out of balance, and at that point, when I moved to London, my male seed was definitely coming to the forefront. I was putting myself very much in control of all kinds of relationships with people to protect myself. I wasn't myself. I wasn't recognising the little girl inside me who was dying to get out, who was fucked up and pissed off. I didn't want to get into it.

It shouldn't be like that, your female seed should be in front because your feminine charms are far more powerful. Why try and be like a man, why? Women are really powerful because they've been given all these coping skills and they've been reared through social expectations to deal with a hard life. Men know that they've got the soft option.

I think I related to a lot of the women who were around in music because they had this feeling of reinvention about them and they were far more explosive as people than anyone else in the business. I reacted far more heavily to them than male artists. Patti Smith gave me this feeling of being a true instigator, a visionary, she really did feel like someone who was special and different. And Siouxsie was like that but she would come out like this bloody peacock, absolutely masked up. And Debbie Harry wore a mask the whole time.

With Nico and Marianne Faithfull the appeal was more on that fucked-up glamour level. I used to listen to Marianne's *Broken English* record over and over again. When you get albums like that you realise the worth of it all in the end, why these people have to go through their battles and why they have to deal with pain. And it all has to come out subconsciously, and I related to that instinct in these women, to that far more animal side in them. I mean I never have any idea why I write or what I'm writing about ever, until I look back at a lyric and then it really hurts me.

When I left for London I went to live with my aunty in Hampton Court for about two or three weeks before I moved in with this manager I'd been introduced to, in Muswell Hill. It was a really grotty flat, but I had a bed and I started to waitress. I lied about my age, because I knew with a bit of make up I could get away with it. I started going to pubs when I was 13, I could always get away with it.

After a couple of years I began playing music with this girl called Christine, and I had a circle of friends and we decided to form a band called The Uncles. By then I'd met the engineer of The Eurythmics album, *Sweet Dreams* and I got him to come round and listen to our stuff, and we were awful, but he liked it. Like Dave, I think he saw the innocence and the naïveté so we made a proper demo and we got a record deal straight away with MCA. It was really unusual.

I met Dean straight after that, because he'd joined The Eurythmics on *Sweet Dreams*. After a slightly embarrassing meeting backstage at Hammersmith Odeon, I met him again in Paris where he was working on the *Be Yourself Tonight* album with Dave and Annie and I ended up joining him and his girlfriend in their band, State of Play.

That band was very intense, we were together every day for a year and a half so when we split up there was a lot of bad feeling. They kicked me out because I was being really, really aggressive. I was starting to really kick then, I didn't know the difference between self-assertion and aggression, and I started to question the relationships between the management and the band. I'd already been ripped off in the past, and Dean hadn't, he was naïve, but I refused to accept it, and decided to use my own judgement. None of them could handle it, as far as they were concerned I was becoming a destructive force, and the management encouraged them to drop me too, so I was kicked out. My money was suddenly cut off, and they had all the equipment and everything. I was having none of it, I went into total caged-animal-in-a-corner mode, because I'd helped get that record deal, and here I was on the rubbish heap. We made an out-of-court settlement in the end and then nothing happened for years. We seriously needed a break, but I always knew I'd work with Dean again.

I've known Dean for about ten years now, and there has to be a reason for him being such an important male figure in my life. It's almost like we have an invisible umbilical cord between us, we don't have to say very much to each other, we can tell how we're feeling by our body language. We're very tuned into each other.

When Dean's mum was pregnant with him, she tried to have an abortion. They got one child out, but she didn't know that she was carrying twins, and that Dean was still inside her. Recently he found out that the other twin had been a girl. He's always had a very feminine side to his personality, but he's always been at odds with it, and now he knows where those feelings come from. And maybe I'm that girl, maybe I'm that other side. We never analysed it, we just accepted it.

Anyway, after State of Play I got a deal with Anxious, Dave's record label. He started to work with me then, which is why I resent this whole protegé thing which happened when Dean and I formed Curve. He was just a mate, I'm really sorry that he was disgustingly famous but he was just a mate! He recognised my strong vision and he knew I needed to develop, even if it took ten years. He was a levelling influence, he realised I kept going past something which needed developing. So I signed to Anxious and did a solo record which was very naïve again, but it taught me a lot. It was the first time I got to work with Alan Moulder, my partner of the last eight years, and Flood, which is the team which now works with Curve. I wrote and produced everything and I learnt so much. I felt so in control, it was like an experiment for me. I learned not to be frightened of technology in the studio.

My solo career never worked out though. The album came out two years after I recorded it and by then I didn't want to promote it because I wanted to do something else. I'd already been thinking about working with Dean again. I was in Los Angeles with Alan who was working with Shakespears Sister on *Hormonally Yours* and I was sitting with Siobhan by the pool writing all this stuff. I had to leave early to find Dean and tell him about my ideas.

I came back to England with my amazing plan! I said, 'I've got the key, man, and all we have to do is shove it in the fucking lock, right?' Dean didn't have any ideas around it at all, so we just went down into the basement studio of the flat I share with Alan one day and he had this little sound going. I said, 'Let's just fuck it over! Everything we touch, it's got to be ugly, it can't be nice!' Obviously that's how I was feeling about myself inside. Because of all the problems of my past welling up inside me, I'd got to the point where I was having difficulty sitting in a room by myself. I couldn't feel, I loathed myself and everything was ugly and aggressive.

Anyway, he got this sound going and it ended up being 'No Escape From Heaven', and that was the first song we ever wrote. It just plummeted out of us. All this shit was flying out of us, we were both ready to do that at the same time. I trusted him. It was done with such venom.

Dave had told me that if I worked with Dean again, he'd wash his hands of me. I'd said, 'Fuck you!' But it didn't affect our friendship, and after Dean and I had written four or five songs I played them to Dave on my car stereo at his rehearsal studios. He wanted to release it straight away, so we sent out our first Curve EP *Blindfold* to the music press and DJs and everyone without pictures or anything because I couldn't expect people to accept this music with all the trimmings and the trappings.

It's almost like you can't make it in this business unless you're some astonishing human being, especially if you're a woman, which is why I didn't want people to judge me on my looks before they'd heard my music. I can't be dictated to by what is socially acceptable, it doesn't come into my sphere of anything at all. Why should I be dictated to by a man's idea of what a woman should be?

I never worry about being a woman in the public eye as far as my image is concerned. I don't really give a fuck about how anyone sees me or wants to see me. I just have to give a fuck about how I see myself. I can't run around worrying about other people because I couldn't love myself if I did that, I'd just be deflecting all the time.

I love the idea of glamour and make up. It's a tool, a way of masking something and it's part of my life. I like it and why shouldn't I? I want to capture people's imaginations on a visual level. I think mystery is about retaining the core of yourself and not letting that be judged by other people or letting yourself be put on a pedestal by anyone, because I don't think it's particularly powerful to be a sex symbol or anything. That's very transient. I mean it's very flattering on one level, and I don't want to turn it into a negative thing because it's quite sweet for these young kids to see you like that, but ultimately you're doing it for you. You have to.

I've had amazing responses from female fans about the image aspect of what I do. They say really positive things. One girl wrote me a letter saying she'd seen me in the filthiest pair of jeans and the oldest Jesus and Mary Chain T-shirt and that I was the most glamorous thing she'd ever seen! She'd totally got into the idea of seeing someone get on stage in the clothes they wear every day. And I don't have stage clothes, I may change my top or something, but usually I just go on wearing the same old thing.

All the letters I get are like that. Seeing me seems to make women feel they can do what they want, that they have to find that glamorous element in their spirit, that's got nothing to do with make up. Because you can put on your make up and your glamourpuss clothes, but if you don't have the inner grace it doesn't work. It has to be to do with the psyche. Anyone can put the clothes on. I think I've just brought a sense of occasion to it, because you can only do something if it's in your nature.

I think I really started getting into the visual thing when I began modelling. I got signed up with the top agency in Newcastle at the same time as I got my first solo deal, when I was 14, and I wanted to learn about images and glamour. I threw myself into it, to see where it came from and what I could do with it and I became very interested in the idea of destructive glamour. People like Edie Sedgwick, Marianne Faithfull and Nico looked like marble statues which were crumbling away. There was such sadness in their pictures. I remember one picture of Nico and her eyes are just black pools. You absolutely wouldn't want to be her headshit. They all seemed to have unfathomable eyes. You couldn't read them, they were just too intensely private. So I decided then that I didn't like nice, pretty things, and what I really liked was glamour from the inside. Even if those women had make up on they looked completely fucked, because everything was coming from inside.

I've said certain things about glamour to the music press which have been treated very superficially. The whole thing is very misunderstood, especially by men. I believe that women are born witches and they have all these instincts and feelings and premonitions, but witches have always been seen as dark things, although they're not. If you look back over the centuries, white witches have always been completely instrumental in society and they've always been women. It's incredible. People have said I think I'm a witch, but I don't. I am tuned in to my instincts and my intuition, and I understand the significance of that, and I know that the original definition of glamour was to do with casting a spell. And women do understand that definition on a far more subversive level than men ever could, because it's not to do with men. It's about female power. Me and Siobhan Fahey have very similar ideas about it, although we joke about it like silly little girls as well, because you can't be serious about it all the time!

But I have been serious about it in interviews and it always gets lost. And journalists can make their little judgements, they can slap on their little labels, but they're not me. I can't live by that. No one can take away my right to project myself. I can portray a certain image if I want to and ultimately I gain control and power no matter what anyone says, because all they're doing is setting up things for me to smash down. That's what's challenging. It's my stage, it's up to me what I do. It's futile and fruitless to think, well, I can't let this media distortion go on anymore, because it will go on. Most of it's done by men, most of these journalists are men, and their perceptions are wrong, but all you can do is what you do. It's not them up there on stage. They like to think they're in control, but they're not really. It's the same as releasing a single which does really well, and they're all in there slapping themselves on the back and drinking champagne and saying how right they were. I just say, 'Yeah, it's brilliant' because it's irrelevant. It's about personal gain, not apportioning praise or blame.

There is a real fear of women which is so deeply rooted in the male half of society though. But I have a raging ambition, and I really think rock is one of the only art avenues left for women to have a great effect.

Debbie Harry once said that the only people who can really contribute to rock music now are women and gays, that they're the only people who can have a new impetus in music because of their experiences. Everything has been written by and about men, there's nothing left for them to write. I don't think women making rock music will change the world, but I think we have a massive contribution to make and it's our time now. It's very subversive because it all started off with a trickle of underground artists and then the more mainstream singer songwriters and it's always been there. But now it's seriously coming to the forefront and I really feel there is a fundamental difference now because women really want to rock. I adore Joni Mitchell, but it's just not like that now is it?

In the 1960s there was all this heavy feminism and it was completely ridiculous because it segregated the sexes, and it took until the mid-1980s for it to become something really healthy. Things always take time. Obviously the struggle is continuing, but I think women feel more natural about being and doing now, and more women are doing than saying. It's more instinctive now, whereas in the 1960s things were really forced and self-conscious. Now feminism really is about making choices, it's very one on one rather than a movement. It's to do with who you are inside.

People ask me if I'm a feminist and I say that I'm a true blue feminist. I greatly value my judgements and decisions, they're my power and I know I can shoot the shit with the rest of them and that's very frightening to a lot of men. I'm the classic example of a girl who can spend all night in a pub and not one guy will come and talk to me. It must be in my aura, in my being. Guys would much rather talk to girls who wear Laura Ashley dresses and are nice and giggle for them, than someone who will immediately see them for what they are, who can read their body language.

I have had periods of extreme anger. Women who strike out for change always end up being fucking angry, because that change is like your work. And because that anger is so suppressed in women, when it comes up it's totally scary. You're not prepared for it, you're like a vehicle.

I'm angry about how I've been controlled by conditioning in certain ways, and I've always had to do something about it. Men are beginning to understand that women have harder lives just because they're women, but they're way behind, because they're nowhere near understanding what it's actually like to be a woman in any sort of industry, not just the music industry.

Everyone knows it's a man's world. Women are making in-roads, but sometimes it feels like it's token gestures. To say the sexes are equal is absolute rubbish. And it's a shame because you really feel that things are running on half steam, that you only get half of the picture. Women are the ones who will create the balance of the world structure. Women know that to be completely ecstatic or to have a really good time you need to form close relationships with other people. Men have to learn things that women have known for centuries.

And the hard thing about touring is that you're not necessarily operating within close relationships. I do think that there is a special place that women have to find inside themselves to be able to be in a band and go on the road. I think women, especially women who do it really, really successfully, are usually married, and if they're not their partner's involved in some way in what they're doing. And on top of that I think there's a place that you have to find inside yourself which is a home for yourself. It's like your little home for that area of your life and you protect it and guard it.

I have a really serious problem coming to terms with it because I feel like in all the other areas of my normal life I have such a three-dimensional outlook and I am a three-dimensional human being, but when I go on tour I have to become a one-dimensional person because that's how I survive. A lot of people become rock'n'roll animals and they become completely hedonistic, self-centred, self-motivated and completely debauched, and they do exactly what they want. There's no rules, it's like a playground. It sounds really cynical and I'm not being cynical, I'm just making an observation. You see these people and they're shadows of their former selves and six months later they're just starting to get more integrated again and then they're off on tour, becoming one-dimensional.

I do struggle with it. I feel ashamed, because I've spent tours coked out of my head, walking up and down the bus, going from town to town, not knowing where I am. I really want to be able to go on tour and be me. I don't want to have to become like everybody else, I don't want to be drinking every day.

I came home from the American tour for Curve's first album absolutely numb and utterly empty. I wrenched my relationship with Alan up into total oblivion, because I was trying to prove that the male figure in my life would leave me, just like my father had left me. It's obviously tied up with behaviour patterns. After being dragged round as a child, I had put myself into a situation with my career where I was being dragged around at the whim of the tour, but I understand that now. And I do believe that men and women handle these situations differently.

It's important for me not to feel isolated at all, whether on tour or not. I need that home inside me. The music enables me to gain connections with people on loads of different levels, on any level that they really want, and that's the only way I know how to do it. I'm desperately fighting against being isolated, because I know it could be my future, it could be my destiny. And I don't want it to be like that, and the only way I can do that is with my lyrics, by saying, 'Look I feel like this, have you felt anything like that?'

The whole point of music is communication and it just seems like a waste when bands like Lush and My Bloody Valentine write fantastic lyrics and you can't hear them. They should be blisteringly loud and Kylie Minogue should turn hers down!

When a woman writes lyrics people always justify them on some emotional level, because women are supposed to be these emotional beings, and sometimes you do pour out your total feelings but not necessarily about a man or a relationship. I think very visually when I write. The music is landscape music and it tells me what to do. Sometimes I think I can hear things that aren't there and I end up singing something completely off. But I like the clashing harmonies and the darkness or the lightness of the atmosphere.

I love romance as well, real Emily Brontë romance. I feel like Emily Brontë sometimes! Sometimes I write something which ends up being perceived as quite nasty when I actually meant it to be a truly, deeply-felt expression of love. My lyrics are always twisted because my logic is twisted and I have to struggle to keep on the path of my true perspective because it's so easy for me not to have one. A lot of my lyrics are written in that subconscious manner and they go completely off the rails. They're so honest that they're very difficult to take in.

A lot of people can't go into that kind of depth, they don't function properly, they just skim the surface. I'm completely the opposite to that, if anything I want the lobotomy, I want my life to be simple I want chemical depression so they just have to give me the lithium, I want a deficiency in my body so they give me the pill and tell me it's going to be all right, but I haven't got any of those things. I've just got an intellect and my intellect controls everything. I have had things completely the wrong way round in my body. I carry my feelings in my head and my memories in my body, so my memories are useless and dead and my feelings are intellectualised instead of being in my body where I can feel them. The really difficult thing for me to do is change that round, which I'm intending to do, and have been struggling to do for months and months and months. But the music is my freedom, it really is that effective, and that's why women need to keep doing this because it can be so liberating.

I mean, it's futile to think you can change the world, we're only 20 years into feminism this time round. And this wave will be crushed, but women have to keep coming back, keep reinventing until we're dealt with. At the moment it keeps getting shoved under the carpet, and that's a very male thing to do. Men absolutely won't deal with the problems they're facing. So things get squashed, but they always manifest themselves in different ways. And while it won't all get sorted out in my lifetime, I can do it for me.

And of course I can do it for other women because female fans want heroes. It's as simple as that. They get them from film to a certain degree but it's always dictated by a script. When you're on stage, you're naked and bare, and you've got to be able to do it. And women fans want confidence, heroes. L7, Babes In Toyland, they're all heroes. They make their fans feel confident, as if they could do it too. It's all to do with sex and self-expression and self-assertion and self-confidence and self-esteem, and all these things which are lacking in women's lives.

I don't feel any responsibility as a role model because if I did I'd be sacrificing myself and I can't live my life like that. I have to be me. I can't succumb to the charms of fans and admirers. I like it, it's great, but I can't let it overtake me and start worrying about which dress to wear. The fans like you because you can't be dictated to, and that's about being a hero rather than a role model.

For hundreds of years women have been seen in very much lower situations than men in society, and I think that now women want to get back to the Aztec point of view that men and women are heroes and that there's a balance to it. I don't think women want to control, I don't think they want to rule the world, but they do want a balance between the yin and yang and that's all that's going on here, the struggle for that balance.

I'd like to be really optimistic and one side of me is optimistic and full of hope for women in music but I am waiting for the backlash, the tidal wave. I'm just sitting here waiting for it. I could be wrong because in ten years' time it could all be wonderful, but when I think about what's happened in history I don't think it will happen. Things will have to get tense enough for the roots of society to be rocked fundamentally and I don't think it's going to happen because of a few bands, it's got to go right across the board.

Feminism has filtered out to the streets but it needs to happen more. Women have to do it because they want to, not because they think it's some kind of area they should be involved in. They have to do it because as individuals they actually really and truly fundamentally want to do it, even without each other. Women have to feel it without the support of any kind of feminist infrastructure, it has to come down to the individual, it has to belong to the individual. Then no one can rock the foundation because you are the foundation, and not some wacky ethic. It's got to be personal because ultimately the only gain is personal. Hopefully other people will gain from it too, but you can't make anyone do anything and it's a fallacy to think you can. But you can make people think.

Credentials

Band:	Bud
Signed to:	Anxious Records
Managed by:	Raymond Coffer
Past bands:	Incest
	The Uncles
	State of Play
	Curve

Select Curve discography:

Blindfold EP (1991)

Frozen EP (1991)

Cherry EP (1991)

Pubic Fruit LP–Compilation of above EPs, US
release only (1992)

Doppelganger LP (1992)

Radio Sessions LP (1993)

Cuckoo LP (1993)

Kristin Hersh

'*I* was totally unprepared for being branded as a
    psycho depressive chick, I didn't know how to get
    beyond it.'

Kristin Hersh

Weaving spells and spirals with words and music, Kristin Hersh has wrenched songs from her body with a force approaching violence for over ten years now. Stabbing through linear thought-forms with the language of her gut, she twists emotion out of blood and bones, rejecting the codes of intellect in favour of something far less predictable and potentially alarming. The jagged beauty of her songs has driven her band, Throwing Muses, into the flesh of rock culture like a thorn, being sweet and sore and impossible to ignore, while her recent solo acoustic album has unfurled like a spiky flower. Too often dismissed as a 'crazy, psycho-depressive chick', Hersh has baffled the music media with her searingly honest methods and found herself sinisterly typecast, when she's merely striving for a reality in music which she finds absolutely necessary.

Originally from Georgia, Hersh was raised in a hippy commune in Newport, Rhode Island by her mother and philosophy professor father. When she was three, Allen Ginsburg wrote her a poem, and the likes of Joseph Campbell were dropping by for dinner. Isolated and less than happy, Hersh began meddling with music at the age of nine, although it took five years for her real songs to make themselves known to her.

At school, Hersh met her best friend, Tanya Donelly, who

became her step sister when her mother married Donelly's father. The marriage was short lived, but the girls' friendship remained firm, and by the time they were 14 they were making music and playing guitar, eventually forming Throwing Muses with drummer David Narcizo and later, bass player Leslie Langston.

During this time, Hersh's songs were beginning to take over her life. She was having seizures and hearing voices from the songs, and was diagnosed as a schizophrenic at the age of 15. Although she was immediately prescribed heavy medication, she continued to experience the songs as having lives and images which would play out in her own life and the lives of her friends, and bodies in which she found herself dwelling for up to years at a time. They would cause her pleasure and pain, distress and harmony, and existed in another reality which threaded in and out of her own, visiting her then leaving her hollow.

When she became pregnant with her first son, Dylan, Hersh became afraid of the songs, hearing them as Bad Kristin, the girl who would sing and scream and take over on stage. She was frightened that Bad Kristin might harm her unborn baby. Music helped her by netting Bad Kristin, but because the music was Bad Kristin, at the same time it nearly killed her.

In 1990 Hersh checked herself into a hospital, was committed and rediagnosed as bipolar (a form of schizophrenia). Conveniently newly labelled by the medical authorities, she eventually left to develop a life with Billy O'Connell, her new manager and partner, and the man who was to really help save her from Bad Kristin. By literally counting Hersh down, talking to Bad Kristin and then counting her out again, O'Connell has helped to stabilise the force which terrorised his wife for so long.

These days Hersh hears the songs as songs, and catches them

into music. She has a second child with O'Connell, Ryder, and continues to play with Throwing Muses, although Donelly has left to front her own band, Belly. Hersh has also made her most positive album to date, *Hips and Makers*, a solo acoustic journey which deals with love and all its complexities.

While Hersh has been hailed as a songwriting genius with dark and brooding talent, her intrigue has too often been simplified as madness. In dealing openly with the media about her perceptions, her sickness and her experience of music, she has hidden nothing, yet the intensity of her songs has re-energised a tradition of female emotion in Western culture, tying up women's bodies neatly with insanity. Suppressed women who reacted physically to their predicaments were coolly written off less than a hundred years ago, and the image of the crazy chick is still part of the scar tissue.

In another time or place, Hersh might have been hailed as a prophet, a soothsayer or a visionary. Male rock stars today who exhibit eccentric or addictive tendencies are seen as heroes and geniuses. Yet Hersh has to fight to be seen in a positive light which isn't overshadowed by the myths of mental illness.

In confronting the traditional structures of music, in questioning the conflicts of feminism, and in challenging the images of women which society creates, Hersh has proved that she is much more than just a psycho lady. She has forged a new and very female language, has learnt to live with her songs and, through the music, has found a way to loosen the chains which restrict women's lives and bodies every day.

Kristin Hersh

I'm from Georgia and my family's from the Tennessee mountains, and while we were down South, my father would play me these depression era Southern mountain songs. They were Celtic in origin so they're in minor key, and they're whiny and dreamlike. I could never figure out if they were dreamlike because the people wrote them when they were drunk or starving, or because they lived in the mountains by themselves. They're also very down to earth. So my dad played them to me my whole life, and then he taught me how to play a few chords on the guitar when I was about nine.

I used to get really frustrated because he only knew a couple of chords, and I'd say, 'Well, now the song should shoot off here and it should sound kind of happy, so then it should turn ...' and I was describing chords, but I didn't know it! I was driving him crazy so one day he just handed me the guitar and I started making up chords, and the first songs I wrote were very, very terrible. Someone asked me if I was a child prodigy recently and I was like 'No!' It was a hobby for a real long time, but a great hobby.

It wasn't until about five years later that I started really trying to write, and then the songs kind of took a life of their own. I can't actually remember the first time it happened. I just gradually realised that the songs were of a different reality and they were getting bigger than me and bossing me around and talking to me all the time. They'd make me do things like drive at night with my headlights off. And then they'd be gone, or they'd jump out in front of the car. It was confusing. I don't remember it very well because I was soon put on heavy medication, and then I would think something that didn't make sense and it would just go out of my head. All I remember is getting on buses over and over again in this kind of cloud.

It was hard, because when you're a kid you have all these ideas about who you'll be when you grow up, and you have all these plans and you think it's all going to work out and you're going to be really smart. And instead, they said to me, 'Well, you're going to get crazier and crazier from now on.' I was diagnosed as schizophrenic when I was 15, although later the diagnosis was changed to bipolar. So that was the kind of grown up I turned out to be!

They have to tell you those things because you're supposed to bring in all your family members and they have to know how to deal with you, which medication's appropriate for you and what to look out for. When you hallucinate they don't really know what's going on, but with me it didn't take the course they said it would.

I always believed everything they said to me, and that was hard. It's good that we have a medical establishment and drugs, but I could never leave my own perception through force of will, because I just was never going to! I couldn't plan to adopt their ideas. When they told me I was hearing things that weren't there, I always said, 'Well, no, you're not hearing things that *are* there!' Which isn't a good argument as far as the medical establishment is concerned. They just give you more pills! But it really makes sense, and I never have left my own perception. I just don't feel like having those voices in my life, so I take medication.

It wasn't something that I would have chosen to have happened to me, and I didn't have any role models for it. I just had my records and they were my friends because I thought, well, they're in that place and I trust them if they can take care of me, and I'll go there too, but I never asked for this to happen. After ten or so years I still haven't got to the point where I think it was worth it, but it probably was! I just have to grow up a little more before I can really think it's as much a blessing as a curse.

I don't want to sound goofy about it, and it does sound arty in a way, but it fucked my whole life up. Completely. So I'm a little bitter about that. But also the highs are incredibly high, it's like God-sex at its best, and it fucks everything at its worst. So is it a good thing or a bad thing? I don't know.

With my solo record, *Hips And Makers*, I have taken the first step towards thinking that it could have been worth it. Besides my having survived those ten years, it's about taking a particular ride, and that's what the album's title track is about. For most people I guess it happens every day in life, but for me it happens with my songs, and you take this ride, so you might as well take it all the way down or all the way up, or all the way over there, because you always end up at home, you're always the body you started out with. When you know you're just that clay they gave you at the beginning, it's all right, because there's only so far up or down or over there you can go. And then you feel really safe taking that ride, it feels good and exhilarating, and you're not dulled by inexperience.

When you're writing songs you have to use your body and your humanness and all your body's knowledge. It's not just spiritual, it's very, very physical. But usually when we express ourselves, it doesn't come out as physical and spiritual, it comes out as this psycho mess, and a lot of people get stuck in that trap of self-expression. But it's the last thing you should be doing if you're a songwriter, it's selfish!

Women, Sex and Rock 'n' Roll

You should get clean and then you can live in your skin in every minute of the day and listen to the music instead of making it up.

I know people get confused about my lyrics because the songs don't make linear sense and the sentences don't run into each other like they do in conversation. I can't think of anything to say except, 'Well, I can't think of better words than the ones I've used. If I could I would have made those into the song!' You can't sum it all up in your brain, it's not right.

I never use filler words. I mean I hate having to say 'I' because I feel like a listener when it comes to the songs, as I've said. But they always tell a story, it's not like they're fragments thrown together, which a lot of people see them as. They just tell a story without specifics that would limit the story. The words are very sweaty, colour, action words. Gut words, not brain words. A song has a real body. It moves and changes and you could adopt it and live in it for a while. I've seen songs happen to me and to other people, and sometimes I've lived in them for years. The whole *House Tornado* record happened to me years after we recorded it. The songs are real. I don't know what other body to say they have, because I've only heard them as songs but they have heat and electricity and images, and that's all we have. That's the only reason we're here.

Maybe the fact that I'm more responsive to the songs in a physical way is because I'm female. Female physicality is a much more cyclical energy. Men are just allowed to be their physicality so it's less confusing. Although men do have a very untapped and there-fore untainted feminine side, and I find they're extremely responsive to lady songs. I don't like to limit the songs to a gender, but in a way *Hips And Makers* especially is just a bunch of lady stories, and men open up to it completely and take it in and feel it. Women sometimes have a harder time peeling away all the layers to get to that and to say it's OK, and that they understand it, and say that they're like that or not like that. It seems to be much more complex for women, and I don't know if that's because women are introduced to shame really early on.

And for women, physicality really comes into it. It's a really heavy thing, because we have a lot of access to our bodies, we can't help it. Our bodies change every day, they're so malleable and so attractive and so out of control. Men have very controlled bodies, but we have chemicals, water, everything's just swimming around in there and it's so perfect, it's so magic, that the best thing we can do is let go.

There are a lot of women who never get used to their bodies changing every day though. And those women, along with all those men who don't know what it's like, call you crazy if you get too intense about it, because it looks like you're spontaneous. If women think all the time, rather than just feel, it gets really difficult. The feminist battle really is a big deal that way. All of us feminists vacillate between saying, 'Well, we can do that because we're as good as men, so we can be like men!' and going, 'Well, wait, we can be women because that's a great thing and that's what we should be fighting for!'

But there's no good pictures of women, so neither men nor women can see women clearly. We don't have a tradition to follow, so we don't know how to act. If we all had mothers and grandmothers who were honest in their skin and did what felt good to them and didn't hurt people and were honest and fair and not sick, then we would all be OK. We would know how to help each other, instead of looking at all these sick people and wondering who to act like, and who's going to hurt us. We could all be so much healthier. But the only famous women we all look at are usually very one-dimensional as far as their characters go.

Women are funny and goofy and strong and weak and sexy and ugly and all these great things and no one sees anything but weird manikins. Probably some anorexic Amazons in trendy clothes are all right, but to say that that's what women are or should be or should aspire to be is dangerous. Because it means that when any of us are following basic female patterns, we look spontaneous and breakable, and that alone can make you crazy.

I've done fashion shoots and I've met some of these fashion people and they really think they're doing art! They're awful, evil people. I've known people who have died of anorexia, and I know it has more to do with what was deep inside of them than what was on the magazine covers, but it doesn't help that the outside world is looking at the magazine covers, because the outside world is such a big influence. To know that there are people making rules who really want you to disappear, who want less of your body in the world and less of everybody like you in the world, has got to break your heart.

It's very hard to fight the image thing if you're a woman making music. People really have to be able to understand you to allow you to do it, but if you're a little bit confusing, you're disappeared. They can't market you, so you don't appear to the public, so you don't have a voice. And that's the most dangerous thing because women are confusing and femaleness is confusing. Real people are confusing.

I was talking to Michael Stipe who sings with REM and he says it happens to men, especially to someone like him who is almost gender free. But he hasn't been disappeared. I have, because for years I gave the press ugly pictures of myself which would make me cringe I'd think, well, here's one for the dogs, we're the ones who make good music. And I didn't exist! I got my foot in the door with the music, but then when I went farther than that, they'd start up with the angry poetess thing, because they could understand that. And I was totally unprepared for being branded as a psycho-depressive chick, I didn't know how to get beyond it, because I wasn't going to start being silly.

Now I'm either seen as a raving lunatic, a mother of two or a rock star. And none of those things go together at all, but of course in my life it's organic. Of course I play music, I always have, and of course I have babies, I always have. And I'm not actually a raving lunatic, but it's a big part of my life, having to fight this thing.

Last night I was handed this long article about me which went on in all this crazy rock lingo stuff about grunge babeness and how I come from another planet. I suddenly thought, what if all this time these people have known exactly what they're doing and it doesn't make sense, but it works and that's what their job is!

People keep asking me if I've changed my image for the *Hips And Makers* album. They ask me how I did it and why. And I'm like 'What image? I don't have an image. What have I changed? You mean my hair? What are you talking about?' They really think that I said, 'Now I'm going to fake a career move into the acoustic genre. Plug into Unplugged. Take some wimpy little pictures of me and market it!' I mean I put on the publicist's dress because I didn't have any clean clothes, so that's why I'm wearing a dress on the album sleeve and I dyed my hair by accident! I made an acoustic record that I didn't intend ever to release, and all they ask me about is my image!

I was raised without sexism, so when I started Throwing Muses with Tanya Donelly, we never thought about how being female might affect our playing rock music. It's only now that I'm beginning to see it. Musically we've always made female songs, but we've always written separately, otherwise our songs may have taken a very different female turn. We both make feminine songs but she knows how to make things pretty on the outside and I've always skipped that! I guess if we'd done it together people might have thought of us more like The Raincoats, or The Go Gos, but as it was we just kind of skipped the whole gender thing. We were so different in so many ways. And everything we did was with The Pixies, and they had three boys and one girl and we had three girls and one boy, so we just kind of made one gender!

I learned a lot from The Raincoats musically though, because they just presented the idea that real time doesn't exist. They would just bang whenever they felt like it, and when they felt like it was their real time, and that's female time. It's not the same as pop music structure, it's not something you can measure easily and that's the antithesis of musical theory. Writing music is extremely mathematical. Also, as far as pitch goes, there's more maths going on, there's a lot of rule-following. But like I said, women know what changing is, so they seem, when left to their own devices, to be underneath pitch and winding around pitch, and so they just remove all of the numbers. So there's no real time, they're just building a body that seems fragile and spontaneous again, and it seems crazy, but it's not.

I get really bored listening to very male music actually. Except that women pay such attention to detail sometimes that they don't seem able to look up and move enough. I like the way men always seem to have an eye to the outside world, and move all the time, and women seem to be so focussed on these little teeny details, that sometimes there's not enough pounding which women are so good at. They're not physical enough sometimes. They're too careful I guess.

It makes me feel so alive to be playing hard music, although in the beginning I was scared sometimes by my voice. On some of our early Muses records I sound like a bug about to be stepped on! But people still come to me now, after *Hips And Makers*, which is a very positive, female record, and say, 'Well, you yell, so you must be pissed off' or, 'You're quiet so you must be depressed.' Why would anyone say that?

I think love and happiness are very grave ideas anyway. Love doesn't have a punchline. People who are in love are all jumpy and freaky and scratchy and no one says they're unhappy! And someone who's playing with their baby is going to look like they're possessed because they're not anywhere. They're throwing everything they have into another person. Those babies are perfect and being in love is a big deal and you can't mess around with that. Even screaming is done out of love. For someone to have enough power over you to draw out all your force and make you throw it at them is an act of love. There's never anger without vulnerability and that's a beautiful picture.

I mean I absolutely am a housewife, and there's nothing that has the same hormone thing as that. There can be so much violence and emotion in a house! It's the greatest job though, it's back-breaking, physical work and it never ends, but you do it because you love people. It's great to be giving and giving and giving and no one can take that away from you, although not many women can afford to do it now. A lot of women would love to be able to afford to take care of their kids, but they have to sell pens and lights and whatever instead.

Mind you, becoming a teenage mother was not a very smart thing to do. I was way too young and way too crazy and I was just afraid that I wouldn't be able to take care of the baby. There are a lot of very shocking things about pregnancy. For a lot of women it's the first time they take care of themselves, and there are a lot of chemicals making you do that, instead of feeling the usual shame and dieting and giving in to fashions or working all the time. Nothing gets in the way when you're pregnant, it opens you up physically entirely. It's a hard-time right after you have the baby, though, you become a milk machine and you look very different!

You should get medals for being able to go for six weeks without sleep though. But there is also something very attractive about that hiding in the cave aspect during late pregnancy and then being with the new baby. At the moment I really miss the kids, and I've got such a craving to be sitting in the dark with just the blue light of the TV and this little tiny baby with me. It's so nice!

We're planning on having more kids, but we're not going to do it at the wrong time ever again! Touring pregnant is not good. While we were touring one time, when I was pregnant with Ryder, The Breeders hung out with us for a while, and Kim Deal (current Breeder, formerly of The Pixies) was really cool about it. We played this show somewhere and someone said that we were really good but that I was pregnant so it wasn't rock'n'roll. And Kim said, 'That *is* rock'n'roll! That's what rock'n'roll *is*! That's what it is *now*, dummy!'

Credentials

Band:	Throwing Muses
Signed to:	4AD in Britain, Sire in America
Managed by:	Husband Billy O'Connell and Geoff Trump of Throwing Management
Select discography:	*Throwing Muses* LP (1986)
	The Fat Skier mini LP (1987)
	House Tornado LP (1988)
	Hunkpapa LP (1989)
	The Real Ramona LP (1991)
	Red Heaven LP (1992)
	The Curse live LP (1992)
	Hips And Makers solo LP (1994)

Sonya Aurora Madan

'*I'm* not making Indian people happy because I'm a
troublemaker. I'm a female and I should be married
off by now but instead I've got a big mouth.'

Sonya Aurora Madan

Introduction

Standing on the brink of her career as a singer and lyricist with Echobelly, Sonya Aurora Madan has churned up a storm of interest in just a few months with her controversial songs, her confrontational nature and her startling voice. Having rejected the learned femininity of her Asian upbringing, she has chosen an androgynous image with which to battle the itchy lust of the music industry and downplay the issue of sex, messing with glamorous sex roles merely to make a point, as with Echobelly's first video for 'Insomniac'. Reluctant to be transformed into some kind of spokesperson for Indian women, Madan is keen to divert the questions regarding arranged marriages now they've been asked 100 times. Her media life is young, so far it's healthy, if a little tokenistic at times, because although she is single minded, watchful and as in control as anyone could be, she is already beginning to be aware of how little influence she can actually exert over it.

Madan arrived in Britain as an infant. Racism hit her like a slap in the head and she carried a feeling of difference within her, not fully understanding it until she was an adolescent. Raised traditionally by parents who had her marked out for an arranged marriage from the age of two, she was trained to believe in her beauty, not her brains, harbouring resentment and feelings of intellectual inadequacy until she finally got a place at college to study psychology.

225

Having never been allowed out, with or without boys, at home, Madan's only exposure to pop music came via the radio and *Top Of The Pops*. The idea of singing appealed to her but she never believed she could actually make a living out of it until she met Swedish guitarist Glenn Johansson who encouraged her to write lyrics, and together the pair worked on songs which would eventually form the basis for Echobelly in 1993.

Dodging the desperate time-warp music press contrivance, New Wave Of New Wave, Echobelly's perfect pop songs inspired a queue of record companies to form outside gigs soon after they'd bitten into the live circuit in and around London. Disillusioned with the insistence of more than one A&R man to turn Madan into a novelty sex goddess, Echobelly settled for releasing their first single 'Bellyache' on independent label Pandemonium, but linked up with Rhythm King shortly after they turned up on Madan's doorstep literally clutching the pounds and offering to set up a new label for the band, Fauve (French for Wildcat).

Also, Morrissey, whom Madan's lyrical and vocal styles have been compared with, has proved highly supportive of Echobelly, citing them as one of his favourite new bands.

Currently with the world before her, Madan is utterly confident of her ability to impress it. Having realised that all artists are misrepresented by the media, she has already transcended the niche so carefully prepared for her as little Indian pop queen, and is wringing the life out of pop's more superficial culture by addressing abortion, coupledom, oppression of Fundamentalist Muslim women, and Nazism. She knows she is a troublemaker, she cares, but not enough to stop. Madan's striking and defiant presence is bound to help reshape attitudes towards a culture which has been markedly missing from Western rock and pop music.

Sonya Aurora Madan

In Her Own Words

I was brought up as an atheist, so I didn't have a religious background, but any immigrant child is going to have the typical problems of a duality of cultures, and the funny thing is children are very able to cope with situations like that. You'll always get children playing when there's a war going on. They cope with it a lot better than adults. And I coped with my upbringing as easily as the next child.

From a white point of view, having an Asian upbringing and then going into a Western school seems like a very strange thing to do. It was the norm for me and I didn't really analyse my childhood until I was about 18, 19, when you start wondering why you're on the planet. It was perfectly natural for me to play with my white friends at school and then go home and eat chapatis.

I did have an inner feeling of being different though. When you're a child you need to have a sense of belonging and you strive to fit in because of peer pressure. If you don't, it leaves you open to child cruelty which, I think, is one of the most vicious things in the human personality. And I do remember being in a group of friends once, and one of them was criticising a child for her colour, and then turned round to me and said, 'But you're all right Sonya, you're different.' Children can't tolerate anyone who's different, they can't appreciate it, and that was the main problem, knowing I was different.

It wasn't just my colour which made me feel different though, it was also knowing that I always thought about things a hell of a lot more. I've spent my life daydreaming. People ask me what records I listened to, and I have to say, 'Well, I spent more time daydreaming than anything else, with myself!' I think I spent my childhood in another world. Childlike imagination is something which we all lose and it's the most important thing of anyone's life.

I always loved fairy stories, but I was aware of the female roles in them from childhood because I wanted so desperately to be a heroine. I wanted to carry the sword and I wanted to rescue people. I wanted to be the princesses as well. I wanted to be able to choose my role rather than have it defined for me, that's all.

As an Asian girl it was difficult to choose my role. My parents were reasonably liberal but I thank God that I didn't have a brother because he probably would have had a lot more freedom than I did, and I probably would have killed him! But because there were three daughters we were brought up in a reasonably similar fashion. Not totally. My parents were a lot stricter with me for some reason. My younger sister was brilliant, she just said, 'I've met a guy at school I want to go out with and I want your blessing. I'm going to do it any-way, but do you want to know about it or not?' I didn't think of doing that, and I was basically banned from having boyfriends. It made me very happy for her but very angry for me.

Basically, my parents imposed their values on me far too much and I resent that because it's meant that for the past God knows how many years I've been rebelling, and rebelliousness is a part of me now. My parents didn't have a big family here and they weren't par-ticularly friendly with a lot of people, so our immediate family was our social life. Indian people don't really have a pub culture so they never went out, they hardly ever went for a meal or to the cinema. They basically brought us up, fed us and looked after us and made sure we did our homework.

It was a happy childhood but I had problems with my mother. I don't know what happened to her in India but she didn't know about the menopause and when she was going through it she thought she was going mad and took it out on me in a very physical way which hurt and confused me. I didn't do anything wrong. But Indian girls are valued in terms of their beauty and their marriageability. And I was the one in the family who would make the best choice for an arranged marriage. I had a lot of offers and it was fucking horrible for me. I'm not sure how my mum felt about that. My sisters were OK, and my dad kept out of it but my mother had a very, very hard life when she was younger. She had family problems, and there's a lot of conflict there, and a lot of resentment and now guilt.

The arranged marriage thing was actually quite humorous at times. I remember arguing with my father about going out and he'd say, 'There's plenty of time for that when you go to university!' And I'd say, 'But dad, I'll be a lesbian by then!' We laughed about it! It was frustrating though because I was a good girl, I wasn't going to shag the first guy who came along. There was this distant cousin who they had in mind for me to marry, and I thought he was a real asshole, the way he acted with so-called girlfriends. But his mother got together with my mother and decided we'd make a nice match. I was about 14, 15, and they were trying to encourage me to consider him and it was horrible, but I had to put up with it. And I felt victimised because I was meant to be attractive, and it confused me. My sisters didn't have to go through it at all, and I really resented that. My parents had chosen me from the age of one or two to be the marriageable one, so this role in life was always there. But it's not usual for just one daughter to be picked out like that and I never understood it.

Ironically, my mother later warned me about Asian men. Tradition forced her into trying to arrange my marriage, but she knew all along that it wasn't the right thing for me. In the end she actively discouraged me. She actually said to me, 'Do not marry an Indian man. He'll kill you if you sit on another man's lap, but he'll want everyone else's wife to sit in his lap!' In fact I've never considered going out with an Asian man. I've never even fancied one because of what they represent. It's like having a distant recognition of possible oppression. I've met guys who've been brought up in Britain and are totally Westernised and they still go and marry Indian girls who sit at home and make chapatis for them. And Indian women are brought up to look after men, we're very good at keeping them happy whether we realise it or not. And I've found in the past that I've given so much of myself to a relationship that there's been nothing left for myself. But it'll never happen again. I've actually written a song called 'Father, Ruler, King, Computer', the title of which came from *The Female Eunuch* and is about the half-a-couple fantasy of the patriarchal society we live in. And I'm saying that I don't want to be half a couple anymore.

Being brought up to be marriageable also meant that I was expected to have a glamorous career. I was told that I should become an air hostess, and my father even bought me a uniform! So I never thought it was possible for someone like me to stand up and sing. I just didn't have that kind of confidence. I had confidence in stupid things, sad things, because I'd always been told that I was attractive. I've never had a problem getting a man ever, but I've never really considered it to be that important because it was so easy, and that sounds really horrible but I'm just being honest here. The most important thing for me to be able to accept about myself was that I was reasonably intelligent because my problem was always feeling stupid and inarticulate. And I felt I would never be allowed to make pop music because I just wasn't capable. I mean, nobody even expected me to get into college!

I did go to college, though, and while I was there I met a guy who was in a band and that was how I got introduced to a rock'n'roll lifestyle. He took me to America on tour with him. He was a very emotional character and he completely possessed me, and it was frightening. It was like jumping in at the deep end because he was only the second person I'd ever slept with. I'd been a slow developer, losing my virginity at 19, and I thought being with him was very glamorous, and it was for someone who hadn't been anywhere. It was destructive though because he was a bit of a control freak.

I remember being in a studio with him once and the producer asked me if I was a singer and I thought, oh I'd love to sing, but I said, 'No I'm a student' and my boyfriend just looked at me and said, 'Oh no, she's not a singer, she's my girlfriend.' I'd have loved to have pretended I was a singer because I wanted to sing, but I didn't think that people like me did that sort of thing, partly because of my lack of confidence but also because I didn't have any role models, there weren't any people like me singing. It was very much a Western thing. Only recently have there been any Asian bands. It just didn't happen then. I never questioned my ability, I just didn't think it was possible.

I had no idea of pop culture. Listening to music was so untypical of the household in which I'd lived that it just wasn't normal. I saw *Top Of The Pops* and I remember listening to David Bowie when my older sister got into him, and I discovered John Peel on the radio, but I wasn't even allowed to see a band until I was 17 or 18. I wasn't allowed out at all because my parents were paranoid about the safety of their daughters. That was understandable because when you've been a victim of racism you expect your children to be more susceptible to abuse if they're unprotected by you. But by overprotecting any young person you're nearly always going to suffer a retaliation.

Anyway, I never thought about pop culture or questioned it at all, and I certainly didn't think I'd ever make it. Careers are very important to Indian people which is good for women because things can be very equal in that way, but they have no appreciation of the arts. I think it's the same in any country where there's no social security. In order for you to have any standing in the hierarchy you have to have a job that's valued. To be an artist means that you will have aesthetic value, but you won't have any monetary gain so you won't be on the same level as a doctor or a lawyer. Also Indian people came to England to find work. The higher classes wouldn't dream of coming to Britain because they pay very little tax and they have education. It's the lower and middle classes who come here, and their attitude is very business-oriented but it's a peasant mentality. My father just told me that he didn't care what I did as long as I was successful which really said it all to me. It wouldn't matter to him if I wrote crap as long as I was making a lot of money. He wouldn't care if I was writing beautiful songs but getting nowhere, so there is a part of me which wants to prove to my parents that I can do this.

The other thing about pop culture is that it is a very Western thing. The only thing India has is the film industry which is bigger than Hollywood, but actresses are slightly disapproved of. Actors obviously get away with murder, but for women it's almost a dirty profession, so when I told my parents I wanted to sing they weren't too happy. Despite the fact that in India actors and actresses are treated like demi-gods, it's slightly smutty for middle class women. So really the only encouragement I had was from Glenn and he really encouraged me when I met him. He came from another country, too, Sweden, and as far as he was concerned I was Asian but I was British. So we just started mucking around musically together.

I have to say now that the fact that there's nobody out there like me is the good thing about this, even if it did mean initially that I had no role models. People have compared me to Morrissey and I do write lyrics which include social commentary, sarcasm, and I like to think, a bit of humour, but I don't consider myself to be influenced by anybody. I wasn't really a Smiths fan. I wasn't even into any female singers especially. Although someone once gave me a Dusty Springfield tape and I was really impressed with her voice and the lyrics. I think that women have voices which are far more pleasant on the ear than men. And now I like to listen to other women just to check out my sisters.

In a way though I really don't want to think of sex or colour when I listen to music. It doesn't matter if it's a man or woman or a black or white person in music. It's purely to do with the tune and the emotion you get from it. If you're going to be writing from a gender-specific perspective, then that can make the fact that you're male or female important, but then there's a universal element of pain and there are songs out there which reach out to everybody. To me the beauty of music is beyond aggression, it's in another world. People can fake it, and there are a lot of fakers in this business. And you can get just as much aggression out of listening to John Lennon. I aspire to being in the John Lennon category. I'm not interested in anything else, I want to be telling the truth.

I was oblivious to Riot Grrl when it happened because it didn't seem to be telling the truth. Basically it wasn't saying anything to me. Standing up and playing a guitar and being female just doesn't come into it because you don't need a pair of tits to play the guitar, you need a pair of hands. And a few choruses. Anyone can do it. If you want to talk about real problems then you should do it, which is why I wrote 'Give Her A Gun'. It's about empowerment for Muslim women and it's a volatile lyric, but deliberately so. When I wrote it the anger and the expression of that anger was more important to me than what I should or shouldn't be saying, but now I am aware that I could be shot by a fundamentalist Muslim or a skinhead for singing it! When Echobelly become more important it will give me trouble.

This whole Salman Rushdie thing has upset me, because how dare anyone threaten someone for writing a book? It really annoys me when white middle class fucks say, 'Well, no, actually you shouldn't criticise that' because what do they know? If the fundamentalists had their way we'd all be in purdah and we wouldn't be allowed out. We'd be treated as ornaments. Freedom is the only choice, and that includes abortion rights and everything.

I know I'm fighting both sides. I'm not making Indian people happy because I'm a troublemaker. I'm a female and I should be married off by now but instead I've got a big mouth. And at the same time I'm using nationalist and racist symbols and throwing them back in people's faces. I get great pleasure from taking and subverting elements of anything which is supposed to belong to people and then fucking it up because it really annoys people. I wore this T-shirt with the Union Jack on it and I wrote 'My Country Too' across the front for a photo shoot once, and then of course the guys in the band have their skinhead haircuts and we're the most anti-racist band around! I just think it's important to take people's symbols and destroy them. It does piss people off but it's good to get attention like that.

It's actually very easy to get attention with dress in that way or in any way as I realised when we were making our video for 'Insomniac'. I had on a red dress with a slit up the side, loads of make up, a blonde wig and high heels, and I was really flirting with the camera, in between being this hard kickboxing woman who's challenging the camera and this slightly androgynous creature with *Blade Runner* robot make up on. Wearing the red dress did make me realise how easy it is to get male attention, because at one point I was rolling around on these satin sheets and the director actually got a hard on. It was quite frightening for me to see how easy it is to get people off. I mean I was just acting out the part, I was meant to be sick and in a foetal position and not feeling good inside and there was this guy getting really excited about it!

The final irony is that the glamorous figure was just meant to be in the beginning but the guys at the record company liked it so much that they decided to keep it in all the way through. I was quite bemused by that but I should have expected it really. I don't mind though because it's such a strong image and if that's what it takes to get people to look at Echobelly, then fuck it!

There is a power in glamour and joining a band makes you immediately attractive. Everybody wants to be near you because you give out a certain amount of power. But if I was just walking down the street I wouldn't get a second look. I think that the standards for criticising men and women for being attractive or unattractive are so much more lenient for men. Men can get away with ugliness, or what would be considered ogre-like in women because looks aren't on the list of what's important in being male.

The whole image and looks thing becomes so important when you deal with the press, especially when you're a woman. I'm painfully aware of the fact that at least one male journalist from the *NME* would always comment on what I was wearing first and foremost, and then would praise or criticise the band, and it wasn't just because I was fronting the band. And the press have really picked up on the fact that I used to be a kickboxer because it's titillating. It's not because they care, and at the end of the day it's got nothing to do with the lyrics I write, it's just another angle. I haven't even done it for three years! My press depiction is basically completely out of my hands, and I'm beginning to realise how little I have to do with it. Most artists are misrepresented.

The image thing came up when we were first trying to get a record deal as well. We met an A&R guy in the pub and he kept going on and on about my appearance. He was more concerned about how I looked than the songs, and rather than saying anything I tried to change the conversation. But he insisted on talking about the kind of image I wanted, and although that isn't sexist in itself, I felt that he was taking time to talk to me about it rather than the guys. And I resented that. I mean it does matter what I wear in a way because pop music is synonymous with sexuality. It's all about being young and alive and sexy and I've got no problem with that. I just don't want to be victimised or put on another level because I'm not an angel or a devil, I'm just like everybody else. And if I have to keep saying it I will. I weigh less than seven stone so I'm used to having a mouth on me!

I just want people to look at me the way I look at me. I am very aware of the way women are exalted into sex symbols, objectified into certain images or whatever, and it would be very easy for me to do that, so I've been going out of my way not to. I don't even want to talk about it too much to male journalists because you end up giving them token quotes and you can damage what you're striving for. It's different with women because women understand what I mean. I want first and foremost to be appreciated as a lyricist, then as a singer and then as a performer. And then as a female if it's necessary. But in order to detract from the image and blend in with the gang, I wear men's suits in photo sessions, or jeans or trousers. It's very unsexual. But even if it isn't for some people what can I do? I suppose you can only do so much really. Because having said that, Debbie, our guitarist, walked past a group of guys at one of our gigs and they were looking at this poster of me with my two fingers up to the world and they were discussing my shagability!

Then again, the sexual allure in androgyny actually doesn't exist for most men. The majority of men think page three is sexy. In the wider world I really am making steps with my neutrality and you do have to keep it in perspective. We're so bogged down with our own subculture of music and the media and creativity, that we think this is the world, and it's such a small part of it. The majority of the world is truck drivers and office workers, bankers and nurses. It's them who need convincing, not the 'right on' journalists. Sod that!

The whole thing is problematic. I mean I see a band like Babes In Toyland who wear baby doll dresses and have blonde hair and red lipstick and because of the sexist world we live in, which I'm part of, I haven't bothered to listen to their music because of what they look like. That's really bad, because I might really like what they do. But when I saw Polly Harvey, I immediately wanted to hear her music. Unfortunately imagery is a part of pop culture like I've already said. But I don't want to get caught up in that, because if I want to go on stage in a bra and a pair of knickers, I will. And if I get hassle for it, fuck it! I'm a strong person and I'll do what the fuck I want! I'll bear the consequences, and really if Babes In Toyland want to dress like that, well, fine. It is a problem because people think if you're a feminist you should be unattractive and that's unfair. Why can't you be anything you want to be?

I want to have the right to change as a woman, singing and writing as well. Women are allowed to become gentler and more feminine but they're not allowed to become more angry. People think you're faking it when you're angry. I suppose the way to do it is through subtle means. Preaching tends to go over people's heads. A lot of my lyrics are subversive, and people get into the songs because they're nice and catchy, but whether they realise it or not, they are influenced by what they take in media-wise so to be really clever with lyrics means being subtle. Apart from 'Give Her A Gun', which isn't subtle at all, and which I make no apologies for, it's much more clever to make a point about racism, for instance, by singing about a three year old in a playground if you want to get a message across, like I did with 'Call Me Names'.

I don't know if I'll always be this confrontational but I think I really need to get some things out of my system. I don't want to make an issue out of my gender and I never even thought about Asian culture until I started being interviewed but all these things are really rising to the surface now. Racism is actually worse than sexism, it's more personal. In the Western world being a woman is not considered to be such a lowly thing as being black, and no one will admit that because it's not very right on. One can take pride in being a woman, and obviously one can take pride in being black, but black women are right at the bottom of the structure because they're put down by whites and black men. It's very logical because anybody who feels persecuted will persecute someone else in order to put themselves in an elevated position, and the person at the top, the white anglo-saxon male, is having the last laugh, watching all these people fight amongst themselves. It's something the English government is very good at, colonising countries.

I really don't want to be this token platform speaker that people are beginning to make me out to be though, because I'm the only articulate Indian female singer or whatever. Having Indian women at our gigs makes me really happy but it's not why I'm doing this. Pushing a role model situation onto me is in itself very politely racist, but I want to touch everybody. I don't just want Asian girls to know my name, I want everybody to know my name! But I am the only one at the moment, because basically, the only other female Asian band, Voodoo Queens, have fucked it up for themselves, and there isn't anybody else. I mean, they'll never break any ground and I think Echobelly will be a worldwide phenomenon, I can see it and it will happen.

The thing I have to come to terms with now is my loss of privacy. I'm already getting freaked out by freaky guys coming up to me. Someone came up to me at Bristol the other day and I thought he'd come to interview me so I took him backstage. I was on my own with him and although I could have handled the situation I'm not ready for any freaks, and I wasn't expecting him. My manager came in and asked him who he was and he freaked out. He started shouting, 'I just want to fucking talk to her!' I just ran.

The guys were in the pub having a great laugh, and it's not fair because if a girl comes up to them it's not threatening. I'm standing there thinking this is horrible, I don't want to have to cope with this. I was angry and they said, 'Oh don't worry, we'll look after you.' And that made me feel resentful too because I just don't want the situation.

It's all new to me, and I'm going through a very schizophrenic phase because I'm beginning to realise what it really means to be famous. And yes, it's different for women because it's threatening. For a woman everything comes into it from rape to verbal abuse. I haven't had any on stage yet, but if I did I'd kick their head in. I did have hassle once from these three guys at the front of the stage and I just stopped and said, 'You, you're pissing me off! Get to the back of the room, if you want to talk!' And the whole crowd was with me. I was thinking, if they gave me any more hassle I'd have thrown the mike stand at them. I do have these temper tantrums but you have to to hold an audience. Basically, that kind of heckling is a very male thing, women don't do it as much. Men just want people to take notice of them all the time, whether they're on stage or in the audience.

One thing that's helped me a lot is having Debbie in the band. It's very important to have another woman on stage with me and I really enjoy having her around because she's one of the lads as well.

I don't want to put anyone down with what I do, I love men and women, I love people. But the reason I'm more interested in women is simply because women are more interesting. Women have to lead more complicated lives, we have all these varied role models, like mother and whore, which don't exist for men, and so women are far more interesting to anyone wanting to create. We've got everything, we're more beautiful, more dangerous, stronger, we hold the key to life, and the sickest joke of all is that we're the ones being put down.

I do think that in the next few decades things will change for women making music though. This is the era of the female singer songwriter. If you're a good songwriter, obviously it doesn't matter what gender you are, but at the moment there are a lot of women who are very articulate and able to be very good frontwomen, and I think we'll look back on this time as being a period of change.

Credentials

Band:	Echobelly
Signed to:	Pandemonium in 1993, now Fauve through Rhythm King in Britain, Sony for the rest of the world.
Managed by:	Paul Bailey for ulterior
Discography:	'Bellyache' single (1993) now deleted
	'Insomniac' single (1994)
	Everyone's got one (1994)

Dolores O'Riordan

When I was 15 I thought God, if life's all about
pleasing the boys on the corner then I'd rather go
to mass with my mother. It was more fun!'

Dolores O'Riordan

Introduction

Having grown up a committed tomboy, The Cranberries' vocalist and songwriter Dolores O'Riordan is still refusing to align herself with conventional girlishness, preferring to look tough and deliver attitude instead. Her poetic sensibility exhibits itself in lavish lyrical exercises which delve into emotions and relationship conflicts, while her voice wavers between sweet and wild. She has a powerful presence, having chosen to develop confidence at her own rate instead of faking it as a star from the start, and the vulnerability which earned her so much criticism when she first appeared has metamorphosed into a truly human, rather than an unconvincing superhuman, strength. She is not the naïve little Catholic girl from the Irish back of beyond any longer, if indeed she ever was, and in discovering her true sexual self and having survived the press attacks which so traumatised her at the age of 18, she is now fit to live up to her huge success.

Growing up just outside Southern Ireland's third largest city, Limerick, with five brothers, O'Riordan quickly developed an aversion to traditional femininity. She was disturbed by the onset of puberty and didn't come to terms with her physical changes until she was in her late teens. Boys baffled her unless she could relate to them purely platonically, and she could never see the point of trying to impress them sexually.

At school, O'Riordan won national singing competitions and at church she became enamoured of hymns and chants. When she was about to finish school, she auditioned for a Limerick band called The Cranberry Saw Us who were looking for a female singer to encapsulate the spirit of their sound. Against the wishes of her parents, and despite the fact that the band weren't quite sure what to make of her, she joined them as a lead singer and lyricist.

Quickly the newly-named Cranberries seized the attention of the music industry, despite being unfavourably situated in Ireland. Geoff Travis, the man who signed The Smiths to Rough Trade, stepped in to manage them, helped by the press when their first EP, Uncertain was released in 1991. O'Riordan, however, was needled for her lack of confidence. Treated as a fey little innocent who hadn't a clue about anything other than supposedly unimportant rural concerns, she felt cheated and ostracised. Shocked by a world where looks were crucial and sass was everything, she grew depressed with the music scene until America welcomed her with open arms and unambiguous delight.

Since the release of their debut album in 1992, *Everyone Else Is Doing It, So Why Can't We?*, The Cranberries have sold roughly two million copies in America alone and Britain is finally catching up in the reflected glory. O'Riordan still feels a little sore about the British music press, but her songs have proved their worth and she feels no need for any further acknowledgement of her talent.

Due to be married shortly after the following interview (which she gave from a hospital bed after badly breaking her leg in a skiing accident), O'Riordan has finally come to terms with her womanhood and made her mark in music. Growing up under the harsh eye of the media has not been easy for her, but she has battled with the scrutiny and the judgements and won. Far from the fragile, ignorant, sullen little slip she was so unkindly presented as, she now appears as a formidable force with ambitious tendencies. Her sense of independence, her emotional perception, her ability to spin simple tales of love and all its tricky corners, have earned her the right to a platform of her own making, and she's taking full advantage of it. Girls need her example, if only to realise that they needn't put up with patronising bullies in order to come out on top.

Dolores O'Riordan

In Her Own Words

I was very boy-like as a child. I always felt inferior but I knew inside I was strong and I always preferred the boy things in life. To me, coming from a Catholic family, the boys seemed to be able to do anything and the girls were supposed to be more restrained. So it did seem more appealing to be a boy, and I was a total tomboy when I was a kid. I used to hang out with my five brothers and I was anti anything that was girlie. I think it stuck to me when I got older because I started to realise I was dealing with a man's world and I was kind of used to it.

I grew up in a very isolated way. I used to go into the city to see Santa Claus once a year at Christmas and that was it. Most of the time I stayed in the fields. It was really cool actually. Our parents used to let us out playing and I was the baby sister tagging along and the boys didn't like the idea of that so they'd try and get rid of me. They'd shoot me or something and leave me dying in a field for four hours. I spent a lot of time alone as a child, outdoors, and I suppose it was kind of nice because there weren't any influences around. You're just left to develop your own personality and your own strength.

It was terrible when I got older because I hated puberty. It was disgusting, sprouting little boobs and my mother coming and telling me I was going to have periods and me being only 13. I was the only girl in the house then because my sister had left home to get married and live in London, and I just didn't want to be a woman. I didn't want these great big fat things hanging off the side of me called hips!

I suppose I didn't really get into being a girl until I was about 18. I didn't care whether the boys thought I had a nice bottom, or that I had a flat chest, it didn't matter. I thought, God, if that's what life's about, if it's all about pleasing the boys who stand on the corner, then it just doesn't matter. I'd rather sit in my bedroom or go to mass with my mother. It was more fun.

I was into guys but I didn't accept the fact that I was supposed to be pretty and have nice long hair and things like that. It didn't appeal to me. I just wasn't into the idea of putting on dresses. I found it more appealing to play soccer. I got on really well with other girls because there were a lot of girls like me. You'd be surprised actually how few girls want to be sexy at the age of 16, and even if they do they turn out to be unhappy with themselves.

Even when I got older I'd never wear anything above the knee. It just didn't make sense after I'd seen myself as a lad for so long. I couldn't see the point! I preferred to wear jeans and a T-shirt. Now I'm older and I've developed a bit more, I can accept my female side more and I can get into the fact that I'm sexually attractive. I've learned that I can look good and that I can use that a little bit if I want, but I never use it too much. I think people who lack spirituality use their sexuality more because it's physical, but you don't want somebody to be looking at your shell too much if you've got something inside. Your spiritual awareness can get wasted away.

I always wanted to sing. I loved it and I started singing as soon as I could talk. My mother was always singing around the house, too, although I never really noticed that until my fiancé pointed it out to me when he came to visit once. I started writing songs when I was 12. It's really funny looking back at them now. I can't believe that I could have written what I did then. Those songs are like something a 20 year old would come out with! I always took everything so seriously and life was such a struggle. Then again I'm still like that now. Our bass player is always telling me to remind myself that I'm 22 and not 32, but I wouldn't be me if I'd had more fun.

The songs I wrote as a kid were about boys, even though I didn't like being a girl. I had a little Yamaha keyboard with a really tacky drum machine, and I'd be singing these little mini-pops about someone I had a crush on. I remember one guy I really liked who was about ten years older than me and he must have just seen me as this little child. The most sexual it ever got was a cuddle! He never realised I wanted him in any other way. When you're that age you have no confidence at all.

When I met up with The Cranberries, I was still at school. My parents wouldn't let me join a band until I'd finished my exams and they then wanted me to go to university, but I told them that I'd wanted to be a singer since I was a baby and these guys were looking for someone. So I joined and we used to rehearse on Sundays.

The bass player laughed when he first saw me. He kept asking me who I thought I was. They were all Limerick boys and they expected girls to have nice clothes and to be sexy. They weren't the kind of guys I'd normally hang around with at all. Even now I think they're much younger than they actually are.

Boys do take longer to mature than girls, and I've never been able to relate to boys of my own age anyway. So when I first toured with The Cranberries I took a lot of crap on my own. I was the only girl amongst all these road crew and band, and I couldn't really talk to them. Plus there were loads of girls hanging around who I wouldn't normally have had anything to do with. A lot of bad things went down in that first year.

Eventually it was all too much for me and I got so depressed I was actually sick. I had to go to bed for two weeks. I'd gone through too much of a change, from leaving a secure family home to suffering all the bitchiness of the music press and the trouble on the road. I never knew who my friends were because everybody in the music industry is paid to look up to the artists. I couldn't handle it but I really had to balance myself or I'd have ended up in a mental home. To get anywhere in this business you have to be tough and clever. Talent is only half the battle.

I also hated being looked at on stage. I didn't care about singing to an audience but I didn't like people looking at my body. Where I come from, you can just sit in a corner and sing and people are happy to listen. It's more of a mental thing, it has nothing to do with what you're wearing. But suddenly with The Cranberries I found myself being looked at and it was disgusting.

I remember when we first came to London everybody was demanding to know why I stood sideways on stage. They told me I should face the crowd and I thought no, I should do what feels right. It took me about two years to be able to face the crowd, and the press all thought I was this silly little Catholic girl which really pissed me off. I knew I could sing, but just because I wasn't up there going 'Look at me! Aren't I brilliant!' they were criticising me.

British journalists are like stone throwers to me. They're dishonest and sexist and patronising. They just degrade women so much. In America it's much better, but in England they just want to surround themselves with women who can't sing but are prepared to talk about their ovaries. I knew I could sing a damn sight better than a lot of other females out there, but they'd all be up there waggling their little boobs about and screeching away. They'd have all the confidence, but not the voice and I knew I had the voice and that eventually it would pay off. True colours always show.

The problem is women are expected to be sexy all the time and I just wasn't into it then. The press were trying to provoke me into talking about my sexuality and I wouldn't, I wasn't ready to and besides I was an artist and I hated the idea of being a sex goddess. I was only 18 and I was still really a child. It was my first time out in the world and I was feeling my way around. I didn't really accept myself as a woman until I went to America and started getting loads of flowers and boys telling me they loved me and how beautiful I was. And I started thinking, well, I suppose I'm not exactly an ugly pig! But I'm glad I did think I was an ugly pig when I was a teenager rather than thinking I was beautiful because a lot of girls who think they're gorgeous end up really empty as adults. Women who are passed over because they're not slim enough or whatever, should think themselves lucky, because the people passing them over are so irrelevant.

Now I play with sexuality and treat it humorously. I take the piss out of being a sexy woman. I put on this gear and I'm laughing at the notion of it. While other people are pouting and saying 'Take me seriously!' I'm like 'Hey, look at the state of me! Check it out, lads!' I find it hilarious.

It's tougher to do it on stage because you can't really wear a straight skirt and high shoes when you're getting into the performance, but sometimes I go out near the crowd and a boy is staring or trying to touch me and I'm just laughing at him. But it doesn't happen that much to me and I'm really glad about that because it means the fans have respect. They're there to listen to what I've got to say, not to harass me sexually. I don't get a lot of sexual harassment. But I do know that as we get bigger and bigger our fan base will change and people will buy our records because they think we're a cool, trendy band and I'm a sexy chick.

Still, what we do has got nothing to do with tits and ass, we're not a girlie-fronted band. In a way I could almost be a man, it doesn't matter. It's all to do with human emotion and human feelings, gender doesn't come into it. Although having said that I think there are very few women who can sing and deliver true emotion and I suppose I do write and sing from a female point of view because I can't deny that I am a female and I do know that it's much tougher being female. When you get to a certain level you can use that to your advantage, but I do know that men relate to my lyrics very well.

I've always liked women like Annie Lennox and Sinead O'Connor, who didn't have to use their sexuality, who were actually making statements to the world, and even if they were screwed up and backward at least they weren't just standing there going 'Look at my boobs! I'm gorgeous! Buy me!' It's very important to have a message. Since I was a child I've believed that the reason why I've been put on earth has been to sing and deliver a message. And I can't exactly say what it is, but I've always felt it. Sometimes when you look at the world and all its problems and we're here worrying because our thighs are a bit flabby, it's ridiculous.

When I think about the women being raped in Bosnia, I just want to be in a position to do something about it. Rape is the worst crime. If you're shot or nearly killed, you can get over it, but being raped is something which wrecks your head forever. It's something I feel very strongly about but I don't want to say too much about it until the time is right. As a female you are scared to attract attention about certain things because if you cause a big stir in the world you generally get into trouble. The very fact that you're a female is bad enough. But as you get older you do fear less and less and you feel more ready to make your statements. You shouldn't really analyse your art though, if you do you're making a big mistake.

Maybe one day we could play a benefit gig or something. I believe that I've got this gift and I've become popular in the public eye now and I can write a song about anything, do a gig for any cause, and say anything to the press which might make people think. It's something which bothers me because I don't know exactly how to use what I've got yet in that way. But hopefully one day I'll be in a position to really help.

I want to help in some way because I really sympathise with women big time. And I love women. I think every woman is so gorgeous in her own way. Women are so beautiful and emotionally open and we can carry that human life inside, it's amazing. But whatever we do we're always going to be at a disadvantage. When it comes to war, men have the physical strength and the killer instinct and you can see it over the years. And the women are made to give birth, to give life. Men take it away. I know that feminists probably wouldn't agree with it, but I do believe in those human instincts.

Touring around the world as the only woman amongst all these men makes you really notice things about being female. It's the one thing which won't change, the sex difference, and you realise that all the more when you see it happening all around the world.

I have to say that I don't think I could do any of this without my man standing behind me though. It really helps having someone who loves you and understands you, it really brings you back down to earth. My fiancé knows me as me, not as Dolores from The Cranberries, and if I didn't have him it would be so easy to turn into a little shithead. After being treated like a goddess all the time you really need the normality of reality.

And I've realised that I'm not living for The Cranberries any more now, I'm living for me. The band will fit in around my life now. I've devoted the last four years completely to the band and to getting into this position and now I'm here I can control it. It took a lot to get here, a lot of being used, a lot of being treated like crap and told, 'Sing, who cares how you feel, Just sing!' And I had to leave my family to prove a point to them. But I've done it now, and I know that I'm probably going to carry on for a while yet. After all, I'm only 22!

Credentials

Band:	The Cranberries
Signed to:	Xeric in 1991, Island Records 1992–present.
Managed by:	Geoff Travis at Rough Trade
Select discography:	*Uncertain* EP (1991)
	Everybody Else Is Doing It, So Why Can't We? LP (1993)

Lesley Rankine

'*People* expect women to fit into these little slots of what girlies are supposed to be and if you step outside those barriers then you obviously want to be a man!'

Lesley Rankine

Introduction

Infamous for fronting the London-based noise terrorists Silverfish, Lesley Rankine has battered her way into the forefront of guitar-driven rock hell with unbending will and deafening opinions. Her frantic stage stampedes sparked off the Camden Lurch, a body bashing 'dance', and her appearance grew more and more unpredictable as she turned out in dresses and lipstick, dungarees and Doc Martens, with red hair, black hair, and eventually no hair. Piling all of her aggression into her performances, vociferously delivering her feelings and thoughts through the media, Rankine has kicked all existing preconceptions about 'femininity' out of orbit, replacing them with an uninhibited, forceful intelligence which has never been afraid of expressing itself. Shocked by such a tirade of female fury, passion and strength, the music press have called her crude, masculine, hysterical and intimidating for daring to step out of line with tradition. Rankine's unadulterated, assertive sexuality is simply too heavy for them.

Born in Scotland, just outside Edinburgh, Rankine came from a musical family, and was brought up by her mother, following her brother to punk gigs before leaving for London to study art. She began working at the Marquee Club and hanging around the metal rock scene and garage band gigs and eventually joined The Grizzeldas with a friend after answering a classified advertisement in *Melody Maker*. A year later she left, and met up with Fuzz, Chris and Stuart with whom she formed Silverfish. A record deal with Wiija got the band off the ground, after favourable press attention, and two albums later they released *Organ Fan*, their debut for Creation Records in 1992, home of Primal Scream and Teenage Fan Club, amongst others. It was to be their last album with Rankine.

Musical and personal differences pulled the band apart after their final tour in 1993. Rankine began to feel limited and wanted to take more control over her career. Having gained the confidence to wreak her very own havoc, she quit Silverfish during the summer and is now concentrating on solo projects, including an album. She has worked with Irish band Therapy?, and also with Pigface, who are made up of various parts of Revolting Cocks and ex-members of Gaye Bykers On Acid, all bands operating on the fringes of rock.

Rankine's very firmly feminist agenda springs from a well of anger with men. She rails against sexual harassment in the street, in the music business, and in bed, and very consciously challenges commonly-held gender standards. She plays with expectations and attitudes concerning feminine appearances, and has serious views on female anger and sexuality.

Instead of a strong-willed individual who believes in her own sexual and emotional powers, Rankine has been depicted by the music press as an insatiable demon with a male libido and a mouth to match, proving the need for her arguments concerning both female sexuality and emotion. Her demanding presence insists that the dichotomous thinking about male and female passions and appetites be re-examined, while her confrontational performances on stage and off call for full acceptance of female expression. She even believes it might happen!

Lesley Rankine

$\mathcal{I}$ started off life near Edinburgh in a wee village which was really cliquey where everybody knew everyone else's busi-ness, and then later moved to a new town between Edinburgh and Glasgow. We were pretty much a musical family, but me and my brother are the only ones who've turned professional. My brother's a bass player and he usually plays sessions with Julia Fordham and John Martyn and people.

My grandad was the one who started everybody off musically. He used to run a male voice choir in the village, and he would practise on us, organising the family into different singing parts. I think getting started in music for me was more to do with my big brother though. He was in bands by the time he was 13 and I used to drag around with him and go to gigs with him.

We were brought up by my mother. My dad and my mum got divorced when I was a baby; he was the archetypal drunken, wife-beating bastard. But it meant that the three of us, me, my mum and my brother, were really close. I never saw my dad again. You don't need dads. All this stuff about the nuclear family is such a load of crap. I don't think I would have been the same type of person if my dad had been around, because my mother really had to toughen up when she left him. She was really naïve when she married, as most women are, and they're usually kept naïve, and if they live as housewives they never learn anything. So she had to smarten up in order to bring up two kids on her own.

It taught us a lot of independence. You learn not to accept the normal attitudes, like you must have two parents and 2.4 kids to be normal. You learn not to accept all that bullshit and always to question it. And I think you develop a really good unhealthy attitude towards men, you learn to be cynical, but that's realistic. It's so naïve to think men are these nice things who buy you flowers and take you out.

I remember small childhood as being a time of real frustration because all these ideas were handed down to me and I thought they were bullshit. My mother was more protective of me than of my brother, he could go away camping at weekends and I couldn't, so I just used to sneak out and get a slap in the head when I got back. I never wanted to fit into someone else's idea of what I should be, as a girl.

I didn't really have any peer pressure because I was a total loner, and totally anti-feminine. Everyone at my first primary school thought I was a bit of a loony, so that put me on the outside of things. I used to be incredibly shy, and I'd go to extraordinary lengths to avoid talking to people, but I thought all the girls at school were bitchy assholes and that all that nice shrinking violet girlie frock stuff was a load of crap. I suppose I saw it as a threat and demeaning to me. I always liked boys better than girls because girls played stupid games and boys seemed to have more fun. I used to get into regular fights with this tough guy at primary school. I was this unknown thing to him—he wasn't used to being confronted by a girl who was bigger than he was, and I think he was really frightened!

People who don't fit in at school realise they have to be stronger so they develop an extra spark plug in their brains. They don't accept the usual bullshit. When I started my second primary school people were interested in me because I was new, so I forced myself to talk to them, and by the time I went to high school I'd developed a sense of humour. I think I got that from my grandad. He used to make up spoonerisms and sit up with me in the middle of the night, playing cards and pissing my granny off.

I always felt different though, and I couldn't understand why I wasn't accepted just the way I was. I think I was probably a stubborn bastard, though, and maybe I got it from my mother because she was always questioning things as a kid. She would never put up with somebody telling her to do this or that, she would have to know why and then she'd have to agree with them. It got her into a lot of trouble.

I suppose the first music I ever listened to was my mother's records when I was a kid, like The Beatles and Simon and Garfunkel and Joan Baez. But then my brother brought home *White Riot* by The Clash and *1977*, and I thought bloody hell, what's this? Me and my brother used to dress up in our punk gear and tear our jeans up and go and pogo to The Skids at the youth club. I was never really a punk rocker though. I liked the music but when people at school started getting into it and it started becoming a phenomenon, I lost interest.

There wasn't anything where I lived really and although Edinburgh was only about 20 miles away, trying to get back was a real pain in the ass. You couldn't go to gigs because the last bus would leave before the main band went on so you had to sleep rough. I did that once, and I woke up in a bus station in Edinburgh in the middle of January and I thought I was dead! I didn't really get into gigs and music until I came down to London to go to the Wimbledon College of Art.

I left Scotland when I was 18 because I was bored with it. I wanted to get into a band but I didn't have enough guts to get up on a stage. I'd played the trumpet until I was good enough to play in my uncle's brass band, and then I gave it up because I was scared of playing in front of people! I thought if there was anything happening in this country it'd be happening in London, the biggest city in the country. I thought in such a big cosmopolitan city there'd be lots of people with really good attitudes, no prejudice, no ignorance and no small-mindedness, but of course I came down here and found it was basically the same. And that's what I wanted to escape because in the town I'd left people were so thick and small-minded and all their attitudes were built on gossip.

Before I came to London, I'd never known what sexual harassment was, but I'd moved into Stamford Hill and I was getting kerb crawled every night on my way home, and on the street during the day because I was young and pretty with long hair and I was on my own. So I developed a general hatred for men.

I think everybody goes through a phase of not having much confidence, and I think that's why Riot Grrl appealed so much to younger women. When you're that age, you're not very confident and you have no sense of self-security and you're being bombarded with all this sexual shit from men, and you're being threatened by men because you're a woman and you don't have that self-empowerment feeling. So you let yourself get treated badly. Every woman has to learn to come to terms with the fact that today, in this society, most men are dogs and they're led by their dicks and they don't have enough brain to lift themselves above that. And it's very difficult coming to terms with that.

I don't think men are naturally dogs, I think there's very little difference naturally between men and women, but men have their whole sexuality constructed and over-emphasised and over-promoted and blown out of proportion and with women it's completely the opposite. Women are not even supposed to have a sexuality of their own, and they're not supposed to be sexually aggressive. I think it's got a lot to do with why men rape and abuse women. So many men cannot deal with this image of what they're supposed to be. They are supposed to be this big tough thing with a huge knob that goes around devouring everything in its path and men are not like that naturally.

During the last century, obviously society has changed a lot and my generation is the one on from the 1960s, and women are far more independent now than ever before. Our daughters will be brought up with that and men are going to have to learn not to be dogs. They've got deeper and deeper into their own quagmire because they've been allowed to get away with it.

In London I hung about in the metal music scene for a bit and I had a job at The Marquee club in Soho, picking up glasses. It was a very misogynistic scene and because I hated men, I'd smack anyone who gave me hassle. I also used to drink myself stupid and I had this reputation for being foul-mouthed, so they used to get me to kick people out at night. I'd just run round screaming 'Drink up and fuck off!'

I never really knew what the other music scenes were like at that point and I didn't know that the metal scene or the music was more sexist than any other. And I think for the most part it probably isn't, it's just that most men aren't quite so blatant as those metal men are. The funny thing about them is that they're always crap in the sack as well!

I met a girl I was in my first band with on the metal scene though. We used to go and see 1960s garage bands together and we ended up forming The Grizzeldas through answering an ad in *Melody Maker*.

We were together for a year, but I've always had a problem doing one thing for any length of time and I also got involved in a relationship with a guy who was a complete headfuck.

He didn't like me being in a band at all. He would make little digs at me, telling me I was treating people in the band really badly, and I recognise now that that's how men get control over women. A little dig here and a little dig there, so you don't really notice it happening and of course you know that he loves you so what he's saying must be true. And then your self-esteem goes away downhill and eventually he gets you to finish the band.

This one had me completely under control for about three years in all. As soon as I started going out with him I stopped writing lyrics altogether. And as soon as I joined Silverfish, and things started going well for us, the relationship began breaking up. I started to come out of it and to realise that he wasn't Mr Right, because for a long time I was really fighting. I really loved him and I thought I could quite happily live with him for the rest of my life, but he was insanely jealous and possessive and screwed up and he kept making the same mistakes over and over and there's only so long that you can fight for a love like that. It becomes apparent to you in the end that you've just got to cut your losses.

I don't know if the band really helped me leave him, I would have done it anyway. And I had my own niche of friends by that time, plus I'd started college again after a break of four years.

I actually met Fuzz, Silverfish's guitarist, through that boyfriend and then we met up again later at the George Robey pub in London's Finsbury Park. I was beating someone up at a gig there and he remembered me!

You know when you've had five years' worth of shit and putting up with assholes, and this little voice inside you just goes, 'That's enough, it's time to punch somebody 'cos it'll make you feel a lot better'? I don't think I hurt him, I think I freaked him out a bit!

Fuzz, and the others in Silverfish, Chris and Stuart, had already seen me in The Grizzeldas, so they knew I could sing. But I guess they were attracted to the idea of a personality in the band!

I joined Silverfish because I wanted to play gigs. It's addictive and you miss it if you don't do it for just a day. I didn't think Silverfish would actually get anywhere though, but after our first gig we were offered a record deal, and we were reviewed in the music papers and I thought, oh, this is quite fun! Now though, I can see possibilities of working with other people.

I used to want to play with other women, but there are so few good women musicians about. There are probably more female singers than male ones, but with music there's more men actually writing. Men have had more experience, they haven't been restricted to one type of music. Women usually make feminine music, whereas men make feminine and masculine music. It is changing, but I think generally* women are taught to be non-expressive of strong feelings. If there's something fucked up in a woman's life, she thinks she's to blame, but if there's something fucked up in a man's life, he'll blame someone else and you'll never hear the end of it!

I think still, on the whole, women are brought up with the idea that rock'n'roll is a male ideology. It's offputting to women, having so much testosterone flying around, because there's part of it which looks like fun but there's part of it that they know is bullshit.

When a guy joins a band, he's got all these different role models, and it's true that men need male role models but women need female ones and when there aren't many, you're more limited. It's like having one arm tied behind your back. You don't have the benefit of the encouragement of seeing someone do what you want to do.

It's like this big space that needs to be filled before women can start on the same footing as men.

When I see a single female musician, I still assume that she has her music written for her, which is really bad. It does depend on the kind of music, though, like if it's dance music I assume Stock Aitken and Waterman are behind it.

The thing is, though, that so much that's been done has been ignored. Imagine if women knew their history! It's such an insult that men have assumed that they're so important that we have to learn everything about them, and that we are insignificant and we are to be ignored! Sometimes it feels like a conspiracy, but it's a natural thing for men to grow up conceited and arrogant. It's inbred in them. And that's how they keep control over women, because they have to control women. They know women are more powerful than they are— we have babies for a start and there's nothing they can do about it.

I've always felt that women's aggression is suppressed. We're taught through fear and intimidation by men not to fight back and not to be aggressive, especially by men because if we are aggressive, we'll hit back twice as hard. Women have to answer back, and there have to be more sacrifices to take things further. Women constantly have to fight to make men realise their place, to make men see their place, that they share this world with women on an equal footing, that they don't own it and that they don't have any rights over women. And I think women will only get that by stuffing it down men's throats, by being really angry and aggressive and strong.

Men laugh at women's anger, they don't take it seriously or see it as a threat. I can't take that, I just start screaming. I realise I've changed over the years, because I used to get so fucking depressed until I learnt the self-empowerment thing, and I realised I was stronger and smarter and ultimately superior to men. Women have to realise that they have to have this inner strength to get anywhere and it's no good being depressed because that does eat away at you. And also the way an asshole male can get one over on a woman is to affect her like that, to frighten her or to depress her or to insult her womanhood. And when you feel that self-empowerment they can't get one over on you. And when you're in verbal combat with a guy, if you're not frightened or depressed, the chances are you're going to say something which will really affect him. You'll have that sense of humour which enables you to take the piss.

I changed about a year ago because I knew depression wasn't good for me, and also the bands helped me discover my own confidence which I never used to have. Hearing that there's other women who feel the same way about things as I do, having the chance to meet them, and having women come up to me in pubs and saying, 'Oh that thing you said in your interview was really good' has all helped. To begin with I wasn't confident about what I was saying and I always thought that somebody bigger and smarter than me would come and make me look stupid. But now I don't give a fuck, because I know I'm right.

I think the biggest problem with feminism is that it's torn down the old set of rules that were laid down by men, and instated its own about what we can and can't do. To me feminism is about breaking down the stereotypes and the role-playing and the bullshit. But I think it's your own sense of empowerment and security which enables you to do that as much as anything else. I cringe when I use the word feminist because it has such an image. I once asked somebody what it meant, and they said it was the opposite of sexist but it's not really. With the way it's been used and perceived, feminism's almost another form of sexism.

I suppose I saw Silverfish as the way to express myself without the restrictions of any tradition and I found that people were taking notice of me because I had this strong guttural voice and image, so I took that and ran with it. It was just me and it always has been, that I want to push things to the limit and shout about it, that I'm not a freak and I'm quite natural and even if I am I have a perfect right to be a freak. People will try and turn you into a freak because that's what they want. David Bowie and Marc Bolan were turned into freaks because that's what people wanted and people will always try and push that image, and the artists will do it themselves. It's also a protection thing—building up this alter ego. Sometimes I think I have pushed it to the maximum, but I do it just to see what happens. When people started making comments about how I pulled faces on stage and looked like a nutter, I started doing it more. It's really manipulative and I love feeling like that with naïve impressionable people. It's so funny!

Initially I developed my image mostly to avoid any sexual attention and heckling from men in the audience because in the beginning I just couldn't have stood that. It would've depressed me too much and it would have threatened me and filled me with hatred. But I never got that kind of attention. I was glad because the males in the audience would see me as one of the lads, and I think that's how they should see women, as their friends, not just as 'ooh, girlie on stage'. I did wear nice dresses sometimes, but I was usually ratass drunk, so I don't think I had that much to fear!

Nowadays I'm wearing make up and looking nice for photos and videos because I want to, and I think I should have the right to do that. I should have the right to do whatever the fuck I want. I've got nice frilly dresses and I've got dungarees and I wear whatever I like, whether it's on days off or for photos or whatever.

I think it's important to not stick with one particular image, because men still have these attitudes about the virgin or the whore, the bulldyke or the little girlie. I used to reject everything that was traditionally female when I was in my teens and you need the confidence to overcome that because people relate the way you look with what's going on inside your head. When I was working in The Marquee, I used to wear mini skirts and fishnets and high heels, and go round abusing men verbally, so I was a far better feminist then than I was in my teens in some ways!

I think you should always throw a spanner in the works, because nobody should be allowed to rest on their laurels as far as stereotypes go. They should never be allowed to think, well she's got a pair of dungarees on and short hair, she must be a dyke, or she's got a frilly dress on so she can't have any brain, or she wants to get laid. But I could never wear a frilly dress with high heels, I'd have to wear boots with a dress, or I'd have raggedy jeans and platform shoes.

I've spent years never fitting in with what people have told me I'm supposed to be, so I probably don't respond to social pressures the way that other people do. I think I'm sensitive to the body size thing though, because I love food so much. I'm not so bothered by being in photos all the time, but I always think, Uuugh! afterwards and that I need to lose a few pounds. But I'm a pig and a slob and I love all sorts of sensual pleasures and indulging in them, and I'm a total anxiety eater. If I'm happy then I'll celebrate by having something nice to eat and if I'm upset I'll console myself by having something nice to eat. Also I really believe that health is found through eating properly— what goes in must come out sort of thing—and I must have green stuff and this stuff and that stuff every single day, so I'm piling in all these vitamins. Far more than I need in fact!

In my late teens I was pretty fit and slim and when I stopped smoking I gained about a stone in weight, so it's a constant battle.

When I'm touring the States and getting so fat and bloated through living on beer and Mexican food, it's great. I love it so much. But then I start rolling over myself and feeling like a Michelin man and I get a guilt thing about being a pig, and I start worrying that I'm doing my body harm and I'll pay the price in later life.

If I feel disgusted with myself in a picture or a video, that lasts as long as I look at it because I've always felt really strongly that there's far too much pressure placed on women to be thin and I think for the most part that most blokes don't give a fuck anyway. They don't have a clue what cellulite is. Women always seem to be constantly fighting against what they are naturally. And women are naturally fatter!

The thing that really pisses me off has nothing to do with body size though. It's when people think I'm just this mad bastard who goes round kicking things. I don't think anybody is so one-dimensional, unless they're fucking boring. It's over-simplifying everything to think like that. But most of the journalists who write those things are ex-public schoolboys and Oxbridge educated and they don't know anything about life.

I suppose I do play around with androgyny, although it's hard to be so objective about yourself. There's a natural male/female thing in everybody, the yin and yang thing, so it's understandable how androgyny can appeal to everybody. Maybe it's the right way to be, rather than being totally male, or totally female, but the sexes have always been polarised, especially by religion.

In this business, though, if you think of Boy George or Danny La Rue, it's easier for men to be glamorous. It's frowned upon when women blur gender distinctions because women are still supposed to be glamorous and attractive, and so much emphasis is still put on that. To blur gender distinctions for a woman means becoming less attractive, ie becoming male. It's got to change, and when it does it'll be more a case of men and women coming together, of men becoming more glamorous and women becoming less so.

I remember being included in this music paper article once, which said me and the American band L7 were like men, and I thought that was the biggest insult ever. That was like saying that I was ashamed of being female! I think women are vastly superior to men, in character, in morality, in everything. People expect women to fit into these little slots of what girlies are supposed to be and what femininity is and if you step outside those barriers then you obviously want to be a man! And all this penis envy thing is such a load of crap—it's men being arrogant. They want to think that women want to be men because it makes them feel good, and they want to feel superior by thinking women want something they've got. I think that's a load of crap. It's a load of bollocks and I don't think penis envy exists.

I don't think women's sex drive is any different to men's, but there are a lot of women who think that the male sex drive is stronger than theirs. I was amazed to hear my friend say the other day that men do need it more often than women—that's absolute crap! I think men need it a lot more as a way of proving themselves, and they need to feel that a woman needs them and they take it as a sign of a woman's love for them.

I don't think the release thing is true either—that sex for men is a release. Most of the men I go out with, it's just not like that for them. I feel a massive release of tension if I haven't had a good fuck for a while and then I have sex with somebody I really like. But I don't think that's necessarily why men have sex, it's not as purely physical or biological as that, because men have the same emotional needs as women. Men with any brain do anyway.

Men without brains are not only emotionally retarded, they also see women purely as sex objects. I don't think women should have to use their sexuality as a tool for empowerment, but it is the instrument of power we have over them. I wrote the Silverfish song 'Hips, Lips, Tits, Power!' about this idea of men's control of female sexuality, and how they kill what they're afraid of. It came from me wondering about why these violent acts are committed by men against women and that men are scared of women because of sex. Man always kills the thing he loves because he wants control over it, and he wants control over women because women have control over him through sex. The song was always meant to be really positive. 'I am what I am, I know what I know, I like what I have.' I take sex because it's mine and it belongs to me and when I give it, I give it freely, and if you don't like it, fuck off because I'm here to stay! It's like, I understand why men do the things they do, they can't pull the wool over my eyes any more. Women are talking to each other these days, and telling each other why men abuse them. They won't put up with this shit anymore.

I feel like I've got the chance to talk about these things, to say what I think is the truth, especially when I see bullshit in the media all around me. Music is such a strong level of communication and that's something women have never had before—their own level of communication.

With lyric writing, you're constantly going round inside your head unless you're writing stories, which I do sometimes, but only sick ones! I think women have an ability, when they're writing, to dig deep into relationships, that men just don't seem to have. Women can explore their emotions more deeply. Sometimes I worry that I've become too introspective and that I'm going to end up an asshole, but I think I'd probably realise and I would get out of myself and find inspiration from other people if I did.

Sometimes my ideas have been kicking around for years and it's a case of piecing them all together. I suppose most of them are about men and women and sexual attraction and feminism. It's what I think about constantly, although not so much now because since writing the Silverfish album *Organ Fan*, I realised that I was getting to be sort of obsessive, and I made a conscious decision not to let it all affect me so much, or so adversely. I suppose my mind's opened up and I'm thinking about much nicer things, mostly to do with sex because I don't get it very much. All my boyfriends for the past three years have lived in other countries from me so I'm constantly thinking about it!

I'm kind of scared about the future because once women in rock aren't fashionable anymore, what's going to happen? Aren't Babes In Toyland's records going to sell anymore? I'm quite optimistic, though, because I think there's female talent out there and I think it's going to mutate into something else. Maybe if the fashion dies down it'll be a good thing because women will be taken seriously on their own merits rather than getting front covers because they're female. I think maybe that's beginning actually. And as long as there are role models it'll get better and it'll become more established and that's what it's got to be before sexual balance can be achieved— a female establishment.

Riot Grrls pissed me off though. I got this bad feeling about them right from the start. I began finding out about them early on in 1992 because I thought maybe it was a good thing, another sexual revolution or something. But then I inadvertently started slagging it off. I'd just open my mouth and this gut feeling would rush out— 'Wake the fuck up!' I know it was mostly young girls who were and maybe still are into it and if they get a sense of self-empowerment from it, then good. But I just feel they're running around with their heads cut off. I think the best, most positive thing you can do is just stand up and say, 'Well, aren't I fucking wonderful!' in whatever form, shape or comment, rather than saying, 'He's a piece of shit because he's a bloke!'

Men need a female establishment just as much as women do, to acknowledge their female side and to allow them to be themselves, to get away from this male stereotyped macho thing, because that is so unhealthy and dangerous. It would be a much greater help if men in the public eye were more vocal about their anti-sexist views though.

I'm always trying to prove things to myself and I think that's why I am the way I am with my feminist ideals. Now I've done the band thing, which I never thought I'd be able to do, and I want to write my own songs and do my own thing. A band is like a safety net most of the time, and once you have the confidence it's not enough. Next time I want to have complete control!

Credentials

Signed to:	Wiija 1989–1992, Creation Records 1992–present.
Managed by:	Richard Gordon
Past bands:	The Grizzeldas
	Silverfish

Select Silverfish discography:

Silverfish EP (1989)

Total Fucking Asshole EP (1990)

Cockeye LP (1990)

Fat Axl LP (1991)

Organ Fan LP (1992)